Modern
composers

Modern
composers

A guide to the lives and works of the great composers
from Claude Debussy to Thomas Adès

WENDY THOMPSON

southwater

This edition is published by Southwater

Southwater is an imprint of Anness Publishing Ltd
Hermes House, 88–89 Blackfriars Road, London SE1 8HA
tel. 020 7401 2077; fax 020 7633 9499
www.southwaterbooks.com; info@anness.com

This edition distributed in the UK by
The Manning Partnership Ltd
6 The Old Dairy, Melcombe Road, Bath BA2 3LR
tel. 01225 478 444; fax 01225 478 440
sales@manning-partnership.co.uk

This edition distributed in the USA and Canada by
National Book Network
4501 Forbes Boulevard, Suite 200, Lanham, MD 20706
tel. 301 459 3366; fax 301 429 5746
www.nbnbooks.com

This edition distributed in Australia by Pan Macmillan Australia
Level 18, St Martins Tower, 31 Market St, Sydney, NSW 2000
tel. 1300 135 113; fax 1300 135 103
customer.service@macmillan.com.au

Publisher: Joanna Lorenz
Managing Editor: Judith Simons
Project Editor: Felicity Forster
Editor: Beverley Jollands

Designer: Michael Morey
Jacket Design: Balley Design Associates
Picture Researcher: Cathy Stastny
Production Controller: Darren Price

Previously published as part of a larger volume, *The Great Composers*

Jacket Picture Credits: AKG, London (*Still life: Table with Armchair* by Juan Gris;
Bartók; Shostakovich); Performing Arts Library, Clive Barda / ArenaPAL (Glass).

1 3 5 7 9 10 8 6 4 2

*HALF TITLE PAGE: Italian composer
Luciano Berio (born 1925).
FRONTISPIECE:* The Man with
the Violin, *painted in 1918
by the Spanish artist Juan Gris.*

*TITLE PAGE: American minimalist
Philip Glass (born 1937).
LEFT: A product of the digital
revolution — a Virtua Digital
Console mixing desk.*

Contents

Introduction

Around the dawn of the 20th century classical music began to change – Romanticism had run its course and become overly self-indulgent. Several new musical trends began, each of which branched out into new forms of modern composition.

One trend developed in step with the post-Impressionistic art movement exemplified by painters such as Edvard Munch, Wasily Kandinsky and Pablo Picasso. Other composers began experimenting with atonality, in which the 12 notes of the scale were treated equally. Nationalism continued to flourish, and after World War II

ABOVE: Although he disliked the term, Claude Debussy (1862–1918) is most often described as an "impressionistic" composer. His most famous orchestral work was the Prélude à "L'après-midi d'un faune", *based on a monologue by Mallarmé.*

composers experimented with minimalism and the use of electronic tape, leading to the eventual use of the computer and digital technology.

This book begins with a general history of composition, from the beginnings of written musical notation until the present day, and is then divided into two chapters covering the great modern composers.

History of composition

Western musical notation dates from the 9th century AD. Modes evolved, leading to the development of keys, harmonization, Baroque, Classical and Romantic forms, modern atonality, jazz, avant-garde music and minimalism.

The principal people involved in this transformation, and their methods, are highlighted along the way, for example, Léonin and Pérotin's *ars antiqua* and *ars nova*, Handel's *opera seria*, Bach's Baroque suites, Haydn's four-movement form and string quartets, Berlioz's programme music, Wagner's massive "music-dramas", Schoenberg's serial music, Stravinsky's neo-classicism, Stockhausen's electronic music and Steve Reich's minimalism.

The book then charts the lives and times of the modern composers, chronologically divided into the early 20th century and the period after World War II.

The early 20th century

The composer most associated with the Impressionist movement in art was Claude Debussy, who wrote fluid motifs with colouristic instrumental

ABOVE: Charles Ives (1874–1954) is acknowledged as being America's first composer. His works were inspired by "American" landscapes, festivals, traditions and historical events, with titles such as Three Places in New England *(1904).*

effects, likened to the tiny brushstrokes of Impressionist paintings.

Meanwhile the Austrian composer Arnold Schoenberg began pushing chromatic harmony to its limits, creating the revolutionary "12-note system" which was to have a major influence on many successors.

Nationalistically, Europe was represented by composers such as Ralph Vaughan Williams, Béla Bartók and Leoš Janáček, and the USA acquired its first nationalistic composer in the form of Charles Ives, followed

ABOVE: *Igor Stravinsky (1882–1971) was arguably the greatest composer of the 20th century. His electrifying dance music – including* L'oiseau de feu *(1910),* Petrushka *(1911) and* Le sacre du printemps *(1913) – forms a major part of the ballet repertoire. There were many varied influences on his orchestral and choral writing, including neo-classicism, jazz, the serial technique and religious texts.*

by George Gershwin and Aaron Copland. Jazz began influencing composers during the 1920s and '30s, and was taken up in the works of Kurt Weill.

Russia produced one of the greatest composers of the 20th century, Igor Stravinsky, who later lived in France and then the USA. He perfected the neo-classical style, as well as using the 12-note system to brilliant effect.

Music since World War II

From the mid 20th century, composition became more fragmentary than during any former era. Rather than following particular "schools", composers tried to find their own original, individual voices. Important developments included the nationalistic and controversial orchestral works of Dmitri Shostakovich, the electronic music of Karlheinz Stockhausen, and the minimalist approach of Steve Reich.

Other composers were influenced by Eastern music – Olivier Messiaen, for example, who combined Eastern sounds with birdsong. His pupil, Pierre Boulez, became a central figure in 20th and 21st-century composition.

ABOVE: *A mixing desk in a modern recording studio. Electronic studios were first used by post-war composers such as Edgard Varèse (1883–1965), Luciano Berio (born 1925) and Karlheinz Stockhausen (born 1928). One advantage of electronic compositions is that they can be prepared in the studio before being presented to an audience.*

ABOVE: *The French composer Pierre Boulez (born 1925) is Olivier Messiaen's most celebrated pupil. Boulez studied the 12-note technique in the late 1940s, and went on to write a masterpiece of post-war serialism,* Le marteau sans maître *(1954).*

ABOVE: *Composing music has come a long way – from the quill pen of Purcell to the computer of the modern composer.*

History
of
Composition

A beautiful example of a medieval choirbook emanating from Germany, now in the State Library in Gdańsk, Poland. The pages illustrated show the beginning of the plainsong chant for the antiphon Rorate coeli, used in the liturgy for the Ascension season.

Music as a Language

We — are we not formed, as notes of music are,
For one another, though dissimilar?

PERCY BYSSHE SHELLEY (1792–1822), "EPIPSYCHIDION"

Musical composition is one of the most mysterious of all art forms. People who can easily come to terms with a work of literature or a painting are still often baffled by the process by which a piece of music – appearing in material form as notation – must then be translated back into sound through the medium of a third party – the performer. Unlike a painting, a musical composition cannot be owned (except by its creator); and although a score may be published, like a book, it may remain incomprehensible to the general public until it is performed. Although a piece may be played thousands of times, each repetition is entirely individual, and interpretations by different players may vary widely.

ABOVE: *An early example of neumatic notation, from a German illustrated liturgical manuscript.*

Origins of musical notation

The earliest musical compositions were circumscribed by the range of the human voice. People from all cultures have always sung, or used primitive instruments to make sounds. Notation, or the writing down of music, developed to enable performers to remember what they had improvised, to preserve what they had created, and to facilitate interaction between more than one performer. Musical notation, like language, has ancient origins, dating back to the Middle East in the third millennium BC. The ancient Greeks appear to have been the first to try to represent variations of musical pitch through the medium of the alphabet, and successive civilizations all over the world attempted to formulate similar systems of recognizable musical notation.

Neumatic notation

The earliest surviving Western European notational system was called "neumatic notation" – a system of symbols which attempted to portray the rise and fall of a melodic line. These date back to the 9th century AD, and were associated with the performance of sacred music – particularly plainsong – in monastic institutions. Several early manuscript

ABOVE: *An early example of musical notation, a 3rd-century BC Greek song. The letters above the text indicate the notes.*

ABOVE: *Guido d'Arezzo (c.977–1050), who devised the hexachord. His statue stands outside the Uffizi Gallery in Florence.*

sources contain sacred texts with accompanying notation, although there was no standard system. The first appearance of staff notation, in which pitch was indicated by noteheads on or between lines with a symbol called a clef at the beginning to fix the pitch of one note, was in the 9th-century French treatise *Musica enchiriadis.* At the same time, music for instruments (particularly organ and lute) was beginning to be written down in diagrammatic form known as tablature, which indicated the positions of the player's fingers.

Guido d'Arezzo

The 11th-century Italian monk Guido d'Arezzo invented the "solmization" system – the precursor of "tonic solfa" – in which various syllables were used to indicate pitches in a musical scale. He also invented the "Guidonian Hand", in which the tips and joints of the five fingers

were used as an aid to remembering the various notes. At the same time, attempts were being made to indicate rhythm in performance, by varying the length and angle of the tails of the neumes, and the earliest polyphony (the simultaneous performance of more than one melodic line) was being explored.

The modal system

From around 400 BC until AD 1500, European music was built on modes. In the 4th century BC, the Greek mathematician Pythagoras worked out a scale roughly corresponding to the (modern-day) white keys of the piano, and two centuries later this scale was being used by the Greeks in seven different ways. The early Christian church adopted four so-called "authentic" modes (corresponding to white-note scales beginning on D, E, F and G), and under the 6th-century Pope Gregory, four more modes were added for the performance of plainsong.

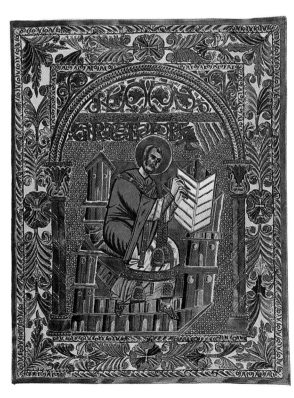

ABOVE: *Pope Gregory (c.540–604), who gave his name to "Gregorian" plainsong melodies for liturgical use.*

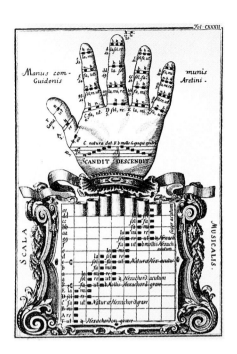

ABOVE: *The so-called "Guidonian Hand", Guido d'Arezzo's device for showing the notes of the scale.*

In 1547, the Swiss monk Henricus Glareanus postulated the theory of 12 modes, giving them somewhat inauthentic Greek names:

> Dorian (range D–D)
> HypoDorian (range A–A)
> Phrygian (range E–E)
> HypoPhrygian (range B–B)
> Lydian (range F–F)
> HypoLydian (range C–C)
> Mixolydian (range G–G)
> HypoMixolydian (range D–D)
> Aeolian (range A–A)
> HypoAeolian (range E–E)
> Ionian (range C–C)
> HypoIonian (range G–G)

Of these, the Aeolian and Ionian modes later became the basis of the minor and major scales respectively, which have since underpinned Western European music. The modes finally gave way to the keys we know today with the development of harmony in the late Renaissance period.

Emergence of Composers

Lovely forms do flow
From conceit divinely framed;
Heaven is music.

THOMAS CAMPION (1567–1620), "OBSERVATIONS IN THE ART OF ENGLISH POESIE"

Much medieval music survives in manuscript anthologies, some copied by monks for a particular monastery, others – often exquisitely illuminated – commissioned by an aristocratic patron. The earliest surviving ones date from the 10th century. Among the most famous manuscripts are two 15th-century English sources, the Old Hall Manuscript and the Eton College Choirbook. There are also two French sources dating from around 1470, the beautiful heart-shaped *Chansonnier cordiforme* and the *Mellon chansonnier*. Many pieces in these manuscripts are anonymous, but some were attributed to individual composers.

Ars antiqua

The Parisian composers Léonin and Pérotin were among the finest exponents of the style called *ars antiqua*, or "ancient style", a method of harmonizing plainsong melodies by adding between one and three secondary voices to the main vocal line, moving in parallel motion. This was known as *conductus*, and was an early form of polyphony – a compositional technique in which several melodic lines are combined, moving independently (as opposed to

ABOVE: An example of the ars antiqua *– a page from the* Jeu de Robin et Marion *by Adam de la Halle (1230–c.1288).*

homophony, in which the voices move together, forming blocks of harmony). European music was dominated by the polyphonic principle from the 13th to the 16th centuries.

By the 13th century, musical notation had become more sophisticated and standardized, with only the finer points of rhythmic

notation still open to interpretation. *Conductus* was gradually superseded by a new form known as the motet, a sacred Latin song, usually with a Biblical text, in which other voices moved in counterpoint to the main tune. The motet has remained a standard form of liturgical music.

Ars nova

At the same time, secular songs, such as those sung by French troubadours and *trouvères*, were being written down. Their flexibility and tunefulness led to the development of a new style (*ars nova*) in the 14th century, initiated by the theorist Philippe de Vitry. The music of the *ars nova*, which flourished particularly in France and Italy, had greater rhythmic vitality, and composers such as Guillaume de Machaut began to experiment with new techniques such as isorhythm, in which the same rhythmic pattern appears in successive repetitions of the melody, but not necessarily using notes of the same value. Many motets of the period were based on this technique, and on a *cantus firmus* – a familiar tune (either a plainsong melody or a folk song) which underpinned a polyphonic composition

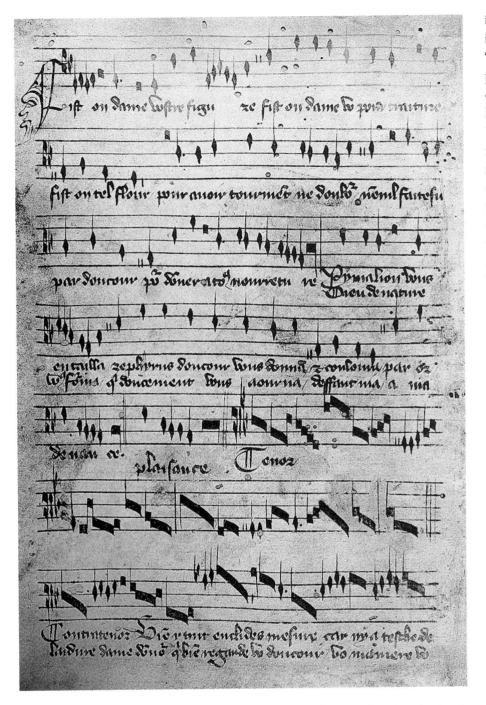

ABOVE: An example of ars nova *notation — an anonymous 14th-century French virelai (song). Note the increasing complexity of the notation.*

increasing sophistication of musical instruments. This was the invention of "monody", a new style in which the old principle of equal voices moving in counterpoint gave way to a single vocal line accompanied by instruments. While the tenor line still carried the main tune of a composition, it was now underpinned by a "ground bass", or *basso continuo* – a strong bass line played on keyboard and reinforced by cello and other bass instruments, which provided a harmonic foundation. The new style – the basis of all Baroque music – originated in Florence, where the composer Giulio Caccini published a famous collection of monodies, *Nuove musiche*, in 1602. The invention of monody coincided with the birth of a new secular musical genre, opera. The concept of a drama set to music, performed by costumed singers with instrumental accompaniment, originated in Florence with early examples by Peri and Caccini. Its greatest early exponent was Claudio Monteverdi.

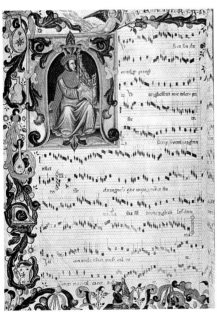

ABOVE: An exquisitely illuminated page from the 15th-century Squarcialupi codex *showing Francesco Landini (c.1325–97) with the score of his madrigal* Musica son.

by appearing throughout, usually in the tenor line.

By 1500 the system of Western European musical notation had become largely standardized, and from then onwards it became increasingly sophisticated and refined. The 16th century (the High Renaissance) was dominated by the principle of polyphony, brought to a height of perfection by composers such as Palestrina in Italy, Lassus in Germany, Victoria in Spain, and William Byrd in England.

Radical change of style

Around 1600, a musical sea-change occurred, partly as a reaction against polyphony, partly as a result of the secularization of society, and the

Baroque Forms

[Opera is] one of the most magnificent and expenseful diversions the wit of man can invent.

JOHN EVELYN (1620–1706), DIARY, 1645

Music in the Baroque era (c.1600–1750) was dominated by an insatiable demand for recreational art-forms. The great aristocratic and royal households, which could support their own orchestras, also employed composers to supply a constant need for new works. In 18th-century Europe, the growing size and wealth of the new middle classes led to a gradual democratization of musical appreciation and the advent of public performances in new concert halls and opera houses.

ABOVE: A sumptuous court entertainment of 1747 in the Teatro Argentina in Rome to celebrate the marriage of the son of Louis XV.

Music and drama

Opera became a favourite entertainment at the many princely courts which dotted Europe; the first public opera house opened in Venice in 1637, followed by others in major European cities. New musical forms were developed to suit the genre, including recitative and aria: the recitative allowed the singer (accompanied only by keyboard) to advance the story rapidly; while the aria, accompanied by the orchestra, allowed for expansive and lyrical reflection on a given situation or emotion.

The Baroque era was dominated by *opera seria*, based on plots drawn from ancient mythology, legend or history, with heroic characters fulfilling their destinies according to approved behavioural concepts. The most prolific 17th-century opera composers included Alessandro Scarlatti and Antonio Vivaldi in Italy, Reinhard Keiser in Germany, and Jean-Baptiste Lully in France.

But by far the greatest exponent of Italian *opera seria* was Handel, who managed to make his characters express real human emotions. His operas have survived, while works by his contemporaries have been consigned to history. *Opera seria* lasted into Mozart's time, but by then audiences were demanding a lighter, more naturalistic type of drama, often dealing with comic subject-matter, which flowered in the hands of Gluck and especially Mozart.

Oratorio

Despite initial resistance, not even the church could remain unaffected by these new developments. A sacred – and normally unstaged – type of musical drama called oratorio, using the same musical forms as opera, but based on biblical stories, came into

being. Most opera composers (such as Scarlatti and Vivaldi) also wrote oratorios, but again it was Handel's fine examples which have survived to the present day. Bach's *St John* and *St Matthew Passions*, relating the story of Christ's death according to the Gospels, belong to this genre.

Instrumental forms

A growing demand for purely instrumental music led to the development of other new forms, such as the sonata. This was conceived both as a form suitable for church performance – the *sonata da chiesa*, which the Italian composer Corelli developed as a standard four-movement form – and its lighter counterpart the *sonata da camera*, which had an unspecified number of dance-like movements. Dance types – gavotte, minuet, courante, allemande, gigue – found their way into instrumental compositions, and their enormous variety formed the basis of the Baroque suite, perfected by Bach and Handel.

Another new form was the concerto, a genre pioneered by Giovanni Gabrieli in the late 1500s, in which a small group of instruments (later one solo instrument) is contrasted with the main body of the orchestra (the earlier form is known as a *concerto grosso*). While Renaissance music had exalted the principle of equality, Baroque music thrived on contrast.

Transition to Classicism

The still, sad music of humanity.

WILLIAM WORDSWORTH (1770–1850), "TINTERN ABBEY"

Baroque music reached its zenith in the works of Bach and Handel. Bach concentrated on sacred music, notably in his many cantatas – dramatic works for voices and instruments intended for church performance; Handel worked in both secular and sacred genres, writing Italian operas and English oratorios. The opening instrumental overtures, or "sinfonias", of such pieces gradually expanded into the 18th-century symphony, which eventually settled into a standard four-movement form with an opening fast movement, a lyrical slow movement, a short dance movement (usually a minuet and trio) and a fast finale. This was the form which Joseph Haydn perfected in over 100 examples, together with another new instrumental genre, the string quartet, written for two violins, viola and cello.

Sonata form

These works, together with the Classical sonata itself, were dominated by the structural principle of "sonata form", in which an opening exposition, usually presenting two main, contrasting themes, is succeeded by a central "development" section, in which the themes are subjected to a variety of treatments. Then comes

ABOVE: A group of musicians playing stringed and keyboard instruments at the court of the Duke of Modena in the late 17th century, painted by Antonio Gabbiani (1652–1726).

a "recapitulation", in which the opening themes are repeated (often in shortened or slightly varied form),

followed by a short "coda" to round off the movement.

Haydn's great Viennese contemporaries Mozart and Beethoven consolidated and developed the symphony and string quartet, as well as the solo concerto – which was now becoming primarily a vehicle for one virtuoso performer. As the 18th-century harpsichord gave way to the more powerful and reliable pianoforte, the piano concerto – and the solo piano sonata – became favoured forms from Mozart's time onwards.

ABOVE: An 18th-century concert with wind, string and keyboard players held at a private Italian palazzo (probably in Venice).

The Romantic Heyday

There is nothing stable in the world; uproar's your only music.

JOHN KEATS (1795–1821)

While Napoleon Bonaparte swept across Europe, toppling the decadent aristocratic rulers of the *ancien régime*, Beethoven's powerful musical vision heralded a new age of individualism. His massive *Eroica* Symphony (No. 3) pushed Classical symphonic form to its limits, while his Sixth (*Pastoral*) Symphony showed how music could be used to illustrate humanity's relationship with nature (a favourite concept of the Romantic era, as illustrated in the art and literature of the period). Meanwhile, as aristocratic patronage declined, the burgeoning middle classes began to demand music on a domestic scale for private enjoyment – a market filled by the music of

ABOVE: *One of the seminal literary works of Romanticism – an artist's impression of Goethe's Faust in his study, painted in 1829.*

Schubert, Schumann, Chopin, Mendelssohn and Brahms, who produced songs with piano accompaniment, chamber music (for combinations of string and wind instruments) and solo piano pieces.

The rapid expansion of the orchestra during this period, together with the invention of new instruments such as the clarinet and the improvement of existing ones, particularly woodwind and brass, led to the creation of much larger ensembles with increased power, colour and tonal range. These demanded new types of music on a vastly expanded scale. In line with the expansionist vision of the 19th century, the symphonic canvases of Schumann, Brahms, Bruckner and Mahler became

ABOVE: *A typical Romantic seascape:* Moonrise over the Sea, *by Caspar David Friedrich (1774–1840).*

ABOVE: An impression of Wotan from Wagner's massive operatic cycle Der Ring des Nibelungen *(1853–74).*

ABOVE: The Russian composer Nikolay Rimsky-Korsakov was the most prominent member of "The Mighty Handful". His nationalistic works include Voskresenaya *(Russian Easter Festival Overture) and the opera* Sadko, *a setting of Russian folk legends.*

ever more inflated; while Wagner's massive "music-dramas", culminating in the epic saga *Der Ring des Nibelungen*, first performed complete in 1876, pointed the way forward to the "music of the future".

Rise of nationalism

While Germany led the musical world in symphonic terms, composers such as Smetana and Dvořák in Bohemia, Glinka, Borodin and Rimsky-Korsakov in Russia, Grieg in Norway and Chopin in Poland were beginning to discover an individual musical culture by introducing the colourful inflections of their native folk music into standard musical genres. Liszt, the Hungarian composer and virtuoso pianist, tackled the symphony from a different angle, inventing the one-movement symphonic "tone-poem" (usually inspired by a poetic, artistic or literary idea); this form was later adopted by Richard Strauss.

For much of the 19th century, England languished as "the land without music" until it was rescued from oblivion on the one hand by the enchantingly witty "Savoy Operas" of Gilbert and Sullivan, and on the other by the genius of Edward Elgar, the first major British composer since Purcell. Italy, however, continued to consolidate its reputation as the operatic centre of the world, with masterpieces by Rossini, Donizetti, Bellini, Verdi and Puccini.

ABOVE: A poster advertising three operas by Gilbert and Sullivan – The Gondoliers, The Mikado *and* The Yeomen of the Guard *– produced by the D'Oyly Carte Opera Company.*

Dawn of a New Age

Music should not decorate, it should be truthful.

ARNOLD SCHOENBERG (1874–1951)

The harmonic tonal framework established during the Baroque and Classical eras remained common musical currency until the turn of the 20th century, when the fluid, impressionistic style of the French composer Claude Debussy began to loosen the hold of tonality. At the same time, the German Expressionist composer Arnold Schoenberg was working independently on a completely new harmonic system, based on the principle of the equality of the 12 notes of the Western scale. Schoenberg's 12-note system, which destroyed the traditional ascendancy of traditional harmony, had many detractors, and he is still considered a "difficult" composer even today, but it had enormous influence on future composers, such as his followers Berg and Webern, and the French composers Boulez and Messiaen.

The innovations of both Debussy and Schoenberg, combined with the raw, exotic harmonies and rhythms of Russian folk music, melded in the works of Stravinsky, the dominant figure of 20th-century music. From his early scores for Diaghilev's Ballets Russes – *The Firebird, Petrushka* and *The Rite of Spring* – to the 12-note music written towards the end of his long life, Stravinsky produced a string of original masterpieces, constantly re-inventing his style to accommodate changing tastes. His compatriots Prokofiev and Shostakovich made significant contributions to 20th-century music – Prokofiev in the fields of ballet, opera and the concerto;

ABOVE: An example of Expressionist art – The Dream *by Franz Marc (1880–1916).*

Shostakovich most notably in his 15 symphonies and 15 string quartets.

Central Europe produced two other major 20th-century figures, both continuing their respective countries' nationalist traditions: the Hungarian Béla Bartók (who was not only a composer, but a major folk song collector), and the Czech Leoš Janáček, whose operas are now acclaimed as masterpieces.

Political events in Europe in the mid 20th century drove many fine composers (including Schoenberg and Bartók) into exile in America. But the USA had its own home-grown innovators: while Aaron Copland and Leonard Bernstein celebrated mainstream American culture in their

hugely popular and accessible works, composers such as Charles Ives and John Cage experimented with new compositional techniques, ranging from aleatory music (which depends on chance) to polytonality (music played in different keys at the same time), and even to complete silence.

As new instruments, including electronic ones, have evolved, new systems of notation have developed to cope with them. In the final decade of the 20th century, many composers abandoned traditional methods of writing music with pen and paper in favour of computer-generated scores, enabling them to produce both scores and parts rapidly and efficiently.

Music of the Future

What we need is a music of the earth, everyday music…
music one can live in like a house.

JEAN COCTEAU (1889–1963), "LE COQ ET L'ARLEQUIN"

The dawn of the 21st century finds so-called "classical" music with many questions to answer. There is no longer any one "system" to follow: the forms and musical styles of previous generations, which formed the bedrock of every composer's vocabulary, have been discarded. Composers now have to either re-invent them, or find an entirely original voice. Some – Harrison Birtwistle, Peter Maxwell Davies, George Benjamin and Thomas Adès in Britain; Steve Reich and John Adams in the USA; Hans Werner Henze in Germany; Luciano Berio in Italy; Sofia Gubaidulina in Russia – are succeeding; others are now seen as derivative or of fringe interest only.

ABOVE: Composition 1999-style, using midi-keyboard and a computer.

Since the 1950s a chasm has opened between "serious" composers and their public. The vast majority of people listen to rock music and other popular forms, and regard classical music as an exclusive and élitist genre, of which they know nothing; while even lovers of classical music often find themselves bewildered by the new sounds produced by contemporary composers, and prefer the music of previous eras. But the 20th century certainly produced its fair share of composers whose music will endure and perhaps in time will become more popular, while young, exciting talents are still bursting on to the scene. And not all new music is inaccessible: as Schoenberg himself remarked, "There is still plenty of good music to be written in C major!"

ABOVE: The British composer Michael Nyman at a 1991 recording session in London.

ABOVE: A scene from Steve Reich's music-theatre work The Cave *(1989–93). Reich's music has connections with pop and rock music, a factor that contributes to its popularity.*

Modern
Composers

The violin repertoire has been enriched by many modern composers: Béla Bartók (1881–1945), Alban Berg (1885–1935), Sergei Prokofiev (1891–1953), William Walton (1902–1983), Dmitri Shostakovich (1906–1975) and Samuel Barber (1910–1981) all wrote concertos for the instrument.

The Early Twentieth Century

An example of post-impressionist art — Woman with a Yellow Jacket (1913) by the German artist August Macke (1887–1914).

Music in a New Framework

*Musical innovation is full of danger to the state, for when modes of music change,
the laws of the state always change with them.*

PLATO (C.428–347 BC)

By the closing years of the 19th century, it was clear that Romanticism had run its course. New trends were apparent in literature and art: in the Symbolist poems of Paul Verlaine, Charles Baudelaire and Stéphane Mallarmé and the plays of Maurice Maeterlinck; in the impressionist paintings of Claude Monet, Camille Pissarro and Edouard Manet, in which representational art gave way to blurred outlines and emphasis on the shifting play of light.

As the 20th century dawned, Impressionism was succeeded by post-Impressionism, and by a bewildering array of new artistic movements: the Fauves, with their bold outlines and brash colours, the Expressionist art of Edvard Munch and Wasily Kandinsky, the cubism of Pablo Picasso, the stark lines of Bauhaus art and architecture. Music, as ever, followed behind, when the focus of new trends moved decisively from central Europe to Paris.

ABOVE: Around the Piano *(1885) by Henri Fantin-Latour (1836–1904).*

ABOVE: An Allegory of Happiness *by Julio Romero de Torres (1880–1930).*

Impressionism in music

In musical terms, composers realized that they need no longer be subject to the tyranny of traditional tonality – a system which had lasted for 400 years. One of the pioneers of the "music of the future" was the Frenchman Claude Debussy, whose fluid structures, built out of the repetition of tiny motifs with colouristic instrumental effects, were likened to impressionist techniques in painting. Little of Debussy's mature music could be said to be in a "key"; instead, its gravitational centre constantly shifts as a result of his use of chromatic harmony.

Atonality

Meanwhile, the Austrian composer Arnold Schoenberg began writing in a lush, late-Romantic style, but in the first decade of the 20th century he pushed chromatic harmony to its limits, experimenting first with atonality, in which the 12 notes of the chromatic scale are treated equally, and then with an original method of musical organization called the "12-note system". This method – in which musical building-blocks are created from "tone-rows" consisting of all 12 notes of the scale – influenced many succeeding composers, including Berg and Webern (who were Schoenberg's pupils), Stravinsky, Messaien, Boulez and Stockhausen. They used it in various ingenious ways and adapted it to their own particular ends.

Nationalism

Meanwhile, musical nationalism continued to flourish: in England in the works of Ralph Vaughan Williams, Frederick Delius and Gustav Holst; in Denmark in the works of Carl Nielsen; in central Europe in the works of the Hungarians Béla Bartók and Zoltán Kodály and the Czech composer Leoš Janáček, the spiritual descendant of Dvořák. All these composers were ardent collectors of their national folk songs, first by transcribing them manually, and then, when phonographic equipment became available, recording them.

The USA – still a relatively young nation – acquired its first major composer in the form of the highly original Charles Ives, quickly followed

ABOVE: Dancing in Vienna shown in a post-World War I painting entitled Once upon a Time.

by others: Samuel Barber, George Gershwin (a populist master), and Aaron Copland, who deliberately set out to create distinctively "American" music.

Music and politics

The political upheavals of the 20th century, particularly the two world wars, had a profound effect on music, as on other art forms. During the economic depression which followed World War I, composers were forced to pare down their musical resources. Works that had required huge and expensive symphony orchestras gave way to small chamber ensembles, evident in the post-war works of Igor Stravinsky and the eclectic group of mainly French composers known as "Les Six".

Another noticeable influence during the 1920s and '30s was that of jazz, exported to Europe from the USA, and taken up with enthusiasm in England, France and Germany (especially in the works of Kurt Weill).

The rise of Nazi Germany in the 1930s struck a grievous blow. The works of "decadent" composers such as Weill were banned, and central Europe was emptied of Jewish musicians, both composers and performers, and of "non-conformist" Aryans. Some – including Schoenberg, Hindemith and Weill – fled to Britain and the USA (where they greatly enriched the musical lives of their adopted nations), while others were murdered. Apart from the aged Richard Strauss, Germany lost most of its finest composers: perhaps the best-known composer who stayed was Carl Orff, remembered only for his popular cantata *Carmina burana*, and for an influential teaching method.

Similarly, in Soviet Russia, Stalin's purges struck fear into all serious composers. The two finest Russian composers of the 20th century, Prokofiev and Shostakovich, both survived, but suffered severely under a tyrannical regime driven by political dogma and opposed to artistic innovation.

ABOVE: L'homme au violon *(The Man with the Violin), painted in 1918 by the Spanish artist Juan Gris (1887–1927).*

This drawing on the cover of The Theatre World *review journal shows Spanish dancers in the 1920s.*

Sergei Rachmaninov

I feel like a ghost wandering in a world grown alien.
I cannot cast out the old way of writing and I cannot acquire the new.

RACHMANINOV

Rachmaninov was the last of a tradition of great pianist-composers, and the last of the Russian Romantics. The dramatic sweep of his music, combined with a haunting Russian melancholy, holds a powerful appeal. His three symphonies and four piano concertos are much loved.

He had his earliest piano lessons from his mother, a trained pianist. In 1882 his family moved to St Petersburg, where Rachmaninov entered the Conservatory. But when his parents separated, he transferred to Moscow, where he studied with the strict teacher Nikolay Zverev, and from 1888 onwards, with Alexander Ziloti (1863–1945) for piano and Anton Arensky (1861–1906) for composition. He graduated from the piano class of the Moscow Conservatory in the summer of 1891, completing his First Piano Concerto at the same time. The next year, his one-

ABOVE: Sergei Rachmaninov, painted in 1925 while he was living in the USA, by Konstantin Andreyevich Somov.

act opera *Aleko* won him the Conservatory's highest award for composition and, shortly after graduating, he wrote one of his most popular pieces, the Prelude in C sharp minor for piano.

In 1897, Rachmaninov's good luck changed when his First Symphony, in D minor, was performed at a Russian Symphony Concert, conducted by Alexander Glazunov. The performance was a disaster (Glazunov was rumoured to be drunk), and the critic César Cui described the piece as "a programme symphony on the Seven Plagues of Egypt". It was not

performed again until 1945. Rachmaninov suffered a nervous breakdown, and could not compose anything for three years. In due course he underwent a successful course of hypnotic treatment with a Dr Nikolay Dahl, which restored his confidence and enabled him to start work on the Second Piano Concerto, the theme of whose slow movement was used to memorable effect in David Lean's 1945 film *Brief Encounter*.

Rachmaninov gave the première of his new concerto, dedicated to Dr Dahl, on 9 November 1901, and a few months later, after finishing his cantata *Spring*, he married his cousin Natalya Satina. Over the next few years he occupied himself with opera composition, until the illness of his daughter Irina obliged the family to move to Dresden in 1906. There he completed his Second Symphony (the

ABOVE: Rachmaninov had unusually large hands, able to cope with big stretches — an advantage for a virtuoso pianist.

ABOVE: Alexander Glazunov is reputed to have ruined the première of Rachmaninov's First Symphony by conducting while drunk.

ABOVE: Red Square in Moscow, with St Basil's Cathedral illuminated. Rachmaninov drew inspiration from the Russian Orthodox liturgy, and wrote some fine sacred vocal music.

slow movement with its long-breathed clarinet solo is a masterly piece of writing), the First Piano Sonata, and the symphonic poem *The Isle of the Dead*, inspired by a painting by the Swiss artist Arnold Böcklin.

In 1909 Rachmaninov made his first visit to America, where he toured with a new work, the Third Piano Concerto. Over the next few years he spent the summers on his country estate, where he wrote the 13 Preludes for piano, Op. 13 (1910), the Liturgy of St John Chrysostom (1910), the *Etudes-tableaux* for piano, Op. 33 (1911), the 14 Songs, Op. 34, and the Second Piano Sonata (1913). During the winters he toured as a pianist, a routine that continued until the outbreak of World War I. His other major compositions of this period include the choral symphony *The Bells* (1913) and the *All-night Vigil* for unaccompanied choir (1915).

America

In 1917, the dangerous political situation in Russia forced Rachmaninov and his family into exile, first in Sweden, and then in America, where he remained for the rest of his life. From 1918 onwards he wrote little, spending most of his time performing. The Fourth Piano Concerto was written in 1926, but when it failed to achieve the success of its predecessors Rachmaninov was forced to revise and shorten it.

In 1931 he composed his last solo piano work, the *Variations on a Theme of Corelli*, followed by the brilliant *Rhapsody on a Theme of Paganini* for piano and orchestra (1934), the Third Symphony (1935–8), and the Symphonic Dances, his last work (1940). By early 1943 he was exhausted and ill, but he continued to tour. He died of cancer at his home in Beverly Hills on 28 March 1943, four days before his 70th birthday.

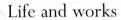

Life and works

NATIONALITY: Russian

BORN: Semyonovo, 1873;
DIED: Beverly Hills, 1943

SPECIALIST GENRES:
Piano concertos, solo
piano music.

MAJOR WORKS: Four
piano concertos; three
symphonies; 24 Preludes
for piano (1892–1910);
*Rhapsody on a Theme of
Paganini* (1934).

Claude Debussy

It's music on the points of needles.

CÉSAR FRANCK (1822–90)

From the late Baroque period to around 1890, mainstream Western music was firmly rooted in Germany and Austria. Not until the late 19th and early 20th centuries did the line of succession stretching from Bach to Mahler begin to branch out, with major composers emerging from Russia, Bohemia, England, Scandinavia and the USA. It was a Frenchman, Claude Debussy, who broke the German monopoly, revitalizing French music with his uniquely subtle art, and opening up a new sound-world for the 20th century. His music explored "the mysterious relationship between Nature and Imagination".

Debussy's life centred on Paris, which was fast becoming the hub of European culture. He was born on 22 August 1862 in the suburb of St Germain-en-Laye, where his parents ran a china shop. The young Claude

ABOVE: Claude Achille Debussy (1862–1918). His unique sound-world opened the door to a new century.

Achille and his siblings were often packed off to their Aunt Clémentine in Cannes, where Debussy began to learn the piano with a former pupil of Chopin. At the age of ten he entered the Paris Conservatoire, where he unnerved his teachers with experimental harmonic improvisations at the keyboard.

Despite his unorthodox tendencies, he won the coveted Prix de Rome in 1884 with his cantata *L'enfant prodigue*, but his sojourn in Rome was not a happy one, and he returned to Paris – where he had been conducting a love affair with a married woman – in the spring of 1887. The same year he became intoxicated with Wagner's music and in 1888 visited Bayreuth. Although Debussy later described Wagner's music as "a beautiful sunset that was mistaken for a dawn", it held a life-long fascination for him. He even began work on a Wagnerian opera, but

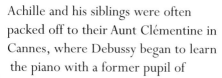

LEFT: Entrance to the Exposition Universelle (1889) by Jean Beraud (1849–1936).

RIGHT: Debussy with his daughter Chou-Chou. He was already gravely ill with cancer when this photograph was taken in 1916.

ABOVE: *A drawing by René Bull illustrating Debussy's* Prélude à "L'après-midi d'un faune" *dating from 1913, the year after Nijinsky's scandalous choreographic version for the Ballets Russes.*

abandoned it when he realized that his own music needed to be "flexible and adaptable to fantasies and dreams".

Impressionism

Debussy had already found inspiration in the elusive works of the Symbolist poets, including Verlaine, whose verses he had begun to match with delicate, ethereal settings. At the same time he began to experiment with new piano sonorities, and with a scale based on whole tones, without a firm key centre. Among his early piano works are a pair of Arabesques and the *Petite suite* for piano duet.

The Javanese gamelan music Debussy heard at the 1889 Paris Exposition left a lasting impression, when he realized that economy of means – a single, shrill clarinet or a gong – could

🎼 Life and works

NATIONALITY: French

BORN: St Germain-en-Laye, 1862; **DIED:** Paris, 1918

SPECIALIST GENRES: Orchestral and piano music.

MAJOR WORKS: *Prélude à "L'après-midi d'un faune"* (1892–4); *Pelléas et Mélisande* (1893–1902); *Nocturnes* (1899); *La mer* (1905); *Images* (1905–7); Preludes for piano (1910, 1913); *Jeux* (1913).

ABOVE: The Great Wave of Kanagawa *(1831) by the Japanese artist Katsushika Hokusai (1760–1849). This print inspired Debussy's symphonic seascape* La mer.

ABOVE: A piece of 17th-century Chinese embroidery. Debussy loved Oriental art, and drew inspiration from it for some of his piano pieces.

be just as effective as a full-blown symphony orchestra. The influence of Art Nouveau, then all the rage in Paris, resulted in his cantata *La damoiselle élue* (*The Blessed Damozel*, 1888), based on a poem by the Pre-Raphaelite artist and writer Dante Gabriel Rossetti.

In the early 1890s Debussy found a tiny apartment in Montmartre, then the centre of artistic "bohemian" life. Surrounded by the artists, writers, fellow musicians, laundresses and prostitutes who constituted the district's lively residents, he set up house with his girlfriend Gabrielle Dupont and embarked on a period of penniless squalor but artistic creativity. During this period he developed his characteristic style, capturing in subtle, shifting harmonies and fragments of melody the essence of a breath of wind, the rustle of leaves, or a shaft of moonlight.

Sometimes his inspiration came from an antique dream-world peopled by masked Harlequins and Columbines playing mandolins and dancing sarabands. These visions sprang to life in the *Suite bergamasque* (1890) for

piano, of which the third piece is the haunting "Clair de lune", the suite *Pour le piano* (1894–1901), and in the Verlaine settings called *Fêtes galantes* (1891 and 1904). From the same period dates the String Quartet

ABOVE: The Scottish soprano Mary Garden (1874–1967) as Mélisande, the heroine of Debussy's Pelléas et Mélisande. *She created the role at the Paris Opera in 1902.*

(1893), and his most famous orchestral piece, the *Prélude à "L'après-midi d'un faune"* (*Prelude to "The Afternoon of a Faun"*, 1894). Based on an erotic monologue by Mallarmé about a faun lying in the grass one hot summer's afternoon in ancient Greece, dreaming of making love to two beautiful but elusive nymphs, the piece – turned into a scandalous ballet in 1912 by the dancer Nijinsky – was a triumphant success. According to the conductor and composer Pierre Boulez, from the first languid notes of the faun's flute, "music began to beat with a new pulse".

In the mid 1890s Debussy worked on the opera *Pelléas et Mélisande*, based on a Symbolist drama by the Belgian writer Maurice Maeterlinck. His infinitely subtle music, economically scored, and using silence as "perhaps the only way of throwing the emotional weight of a phrase into relief", perfectly complemented Maeterlinck's perplexing play, in which the characters seem to lack normal motivation. It took nine years for *Pelléas* to reach the stage, when it was greeted with incomprehension and hostility. It is now recognized as a masterpiece.

During this period, Debussy had lived off a small annual allowance from a publisher. Constant lack of money caused friction between him and Gaby, and the couple finally separated in 1898, just as Debussy finished another orchestral work, the three *Nocturnes*. These poetic evocations of a cloudy day over the river Seine, a Parisian carnival complete with brass band, and a delicate seascape with mermaids singing, are among his most "impressionistic" pieces, as are the contemporary set of *Estampes* (*Prints*) for piano, consisting of the pseudo-oriental *Pagodes*, *Soirée dans Grenade* (*Evening in Granada*, a languid Spanish habanera), and the virtuosic *Jardins sous la pluie* (*Gardens in the rain*).

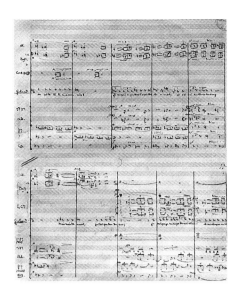

ABOVE: A page from the autograph score of Act I of Pelléas et Mélisande.

Marriage

In 1899 Debussy – whose dark, Mephistophelean looks made him immensely attractive to women – replaced Gaby with a pretty bottle-blonde model called Lilly Texier. Ill-educated and tubercular, Lilly proved an entirely unsuitable wife. In 1903 Debussy met Emma Bardac, Fauré's ex-mistress, now the wife of a banker. They fell passionately in love and eloped to Jersey (where he wrote the piano piece *L'île joyeuse*). Lilly Debussy tried to shoot herself and Debussy was ostracized by his friends, but he and Emma set up house together in the fashionable Avenue du Bois de Boulogne, where their adored daughter Claude-Emma (Chou-Chou) was born in 1905. For the rest of his life Debussy attempted to keep Emma in the style to which she had become accustomed, often with great difficulty, and their ten-year marriage was frequently under strain, especially when he was obliged to leave on long conducting tours.

In 1905 Debussy completed his symphonic seascape *La mer*, a vivid example of his ability to create, through a mosaic of melody and delicate touches of instrumentation, an impression of the interplay between light and water. Over the next few years he also completed two sets of *Images* for piano, the delightful *Children's Corner* (1906–8) for his daughter, two books of piano Preludes, and a set of orchestral *Images*: *Rondes de printemps* (*Dances of Spring*), *Iberia* and *Gigues*. In 1911 he tried his hand at ballet music in *Khamma*, written for the Canadian dancer Maud Allan, and in 1913, in the masterly score *Jeux* (*Games*), written for Diaghilev's Ballets Russes and choreographed by Nijinsky.

Last works

By 1914 Debussy knew that he was mortally ill with cancer of the colon. Deeply distressed by the carnage of World War I, he worked feverishly to finish two sets of piano studies, inspired by Chopin's, and three pieces for two pianos, *En blanc et noir* (1915), each dedicated to a friend killed in action. His last works were three out of a projected set of six sonatas – abstract music in a new, austere style

ABOVE: The Russian impresario Sergei Diaghilev, the driving force behind the Ballets Russes. He commissioned Debussy's Jeux.

– for cello and piano, violin and piano, and flute, viola and harp. He did not live to write the other three, dying during a German bombardment on 25 March 1918. His sonatas were published with the simple inscription: "Claude Debussy: musicien français".

ABOVE: An impressionist seascape – Storm at Agay, *1895, by Jean Baptiste Guillaumin (1841–1927).*

Maurice Ravel

All the same, he had talent, that Ravel.

Ravel

Debussy and his younger contemporary Ravel are often classed together as "impressionist" composers, and in life they sometimes found themselves in unintentional rivalry. In fact, the music of each was quite individual.

Ravel was the son of an engineer of Swiss origin and his Basque wife. When he was a baby the family moved to Paris, where Ravel spent the rest of his life. Like Debussy, he showed early promise as a pianist, and when he was 14 he entered the Paris Conservatoire. During his student days he came into contact with Javanese gamelan music (at the 1889 Paris Exposition), Russian music and Wagner, all of which indirectly influenced his own work.

Having graduated from the piano class in 1895, Ravel returned two years

ABOVE: The French composer Maurice Ravel (1875–1937), painted as a young man by Henri-Charles Manguin.

later to study composition with Fauré. An interest in Renaissance literature encouraged him to set poems by Clément Marot (c.1497–1544), and to write the *Menuet antique* (1895) and the *Pavane pour une infante défunte* (*Pavan for a Dead Infanta*, 1899) for piano; the latter became one of his most popular works. However, his outstandingly original talent disconcerted the Conservatoire's staid establishment, and he failed to win the Prix de Rome five times. Indeed, when he was eliminated in the first round in 1905, having already composed the virtuoso piano piece *Jeux d'eau* (1901), the String Quartet (1902–3), and the ravishing orchestral song-cycle *Shéhérazade* (1903), a huge public row forced the resignation of the Conservatoire's director.

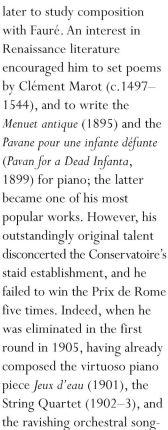

LEFT: Ravel at the piano. He was a brilliant pianist, and often performed his own music.

RIGHT: Ravel's villa, Le Belvedere, at Montfort-l'Amaury, near Paris.

Les Apaches

By now Ravel was a member of the artistic circle of poets, musicians, critics and painters known as "Les Apaches". His tiny stature, his addiction to elegant clothes and his impeccable toilette ensured his social popularity. His sexual proclivities are still unclear, but he never married and remained deeply attached to his mother. With the "*affaire* Ravel" at the Conservatoire behind him, he concentrated on composition, including the *Sonatine* (1903–5) and *Miroirs* (1904–5) for piano, the Introduction and Allegro for harp and chamber ensemble, the song-cycle *Histoires naturelles* (1906), and the evocative orchestral *Rapsodie espagnole* (1907–8). He also began work on his first opera, *L'heure espagnole* (1907–9), influenced by his Basque origins, and in 1911 turned his piano suite *Ma mère l'oye* (*Mother Goose*), originally written

ABOVE: Spanish flamenco dancing. Ravel's Boléro *pays homage to his lifelong love of Spain.*

ABOVE: A design by Leon Bakst (1866–1924) for Act I of the Russian Ballet production of Ravel's Daphnis et Chloé *in Paris, 1912.*

for two children, into a ballet score. From the same period dates his most famous ballet, *Daphnis et Chloé* (1909–12), which was commissioned by Diaghilev.

War years

At the outbreak of World War I, Ravel was working on his Piano Trio. Turned down for military service on the grounds of his size, he became an ambulance driver on the Western Front until his health broke down. The death of his mother in 1916 was a cruel blow. His creative response to tragedy was *Le tombeau de Couperin* (1917), an anachronistic keyboard suite commemorating fallen friends, and the post-war *La valse*, a savage vision of a ghostly waltz to destruction. In 1921 Ravel moved to a small villa at Montfort-l'Amaury near Paris, which he filled with cats, toys and delicate *objets d'art*. His love of children was reflected in his next opera, *L'enfant et les sortilèges* (*The Child and the Magic Spells*, 1925), in which he used a libretto by Colette (1873–1954) to recreate an enchanted childhood world peopled by talking toys and animals. He commemorated Debussy's early death with his Duo for violin and cello, composed the song-cycle *Chansons*

madécasses (1925–6) for the American patroness Elizabeth Sprague Coolidge, and began work on two violin works, *Tzigane* (1924) and the Sonata (1923–7).

Last works

In 1928, the year he visited America, Ravel composed the ballet *Boléro*, whose success came to haunt him. His two brilliant piano concertos (one for the left hand, in F, for the pianist Paul Wittgenstein, who had lost his right arm during World War I) appeared soon after this. His last work was the set of songs *Don Quichotte à Dulcinée* (1932–3), written for a film based on Cervantes' novel.

For the last five years of his life Ravel suffered from Pick's disease, an illness accelerated by brain damage sustained in a car crash. He died in 1937.

Life and works

NATIONALITY: French

BORN: Ciboure, Basses-Pyrénées, 1875; **DIED:** Paris, 1937

SPECIALIST GENRES: Virtuoso piano music, orchestral works.

MAJOR WORKS: *Pavane pour une infante défunte* (1899); *Jeux d'eau* (1901); *Miroirs* (1904–5); *Gaspard de la nuit* (1908); *Daphnis et Chloé* (1909–12); *Le tombeau de Couperin* (1917); *L'enfant et les sortilèges* (1925); *Boléro* (1928); two piano concertos (1929–31).

Erik Satie

My brother was always difficult to understand.
He doesn't seem to have been quite normal.

OLGA SATIE

A contemporary of Debussy and Ravel, Erik Satie was a pioneer of the avant-garde. His satirical, anti-bourgeois attitudes and eccentric demeanour anticipated Dadaism and Surrealism, while his spare, whimsical musical style was the antithesis of late Romanticism. He had enormous influence on the group of composers known as "Les Six", as well as on later figures such as John Cage.

The son of a French father and a Scottish mother, he was born in Honfleur on the Normandy coast, and moved to Paris in 1878. He studied at the Paris Conservatoire, but achieved little success. His early works for piano include *Sarabandes* (1887), the hypnotic *Gymnopédies* (1888) and the exotic-sounding *Gnossiennes* (1890). For several years he earned a meagre living playing the piano in Montmartre bars and cabarets, and also became involved

ABOVE: *Erik Satie (1866–1925), one of the great eccentrics.*

with the occult Rosicrucian sect, "founding" the Metropolitan Church of the Art of Jesus the Conductor.

Around 1890 Satie met Debussy, beginning a 25-year friendship in which Debussy was very much the superior partner, with Satie as his court jester. During this period Satie had a tempestuous love affair with the painter Suzanne Valadon (the mother of Utrillo), and became known for eccentric gestures, such as buying 12 identical grey velvet suits. In 1898 he left Montmartre for the grim suburb of Arcueil-Cachan, where he lived in one small, bare room.

Satie's later compositions often have deliberately obscure titles, such as *Trois véritables préludes flasques (pour un chien)* (*Three flabby preludes for a dog*), *Choses vues à droite et à gauche (sans lunettes)*

(*Things seen from the right and left without spectacles*) and *Trois morceaux en forme de poire* (*Three pear-shaped pieces*), though there are actually seven.

During World War I Satie collaborated with the writer Jean Cocteau (1889–1963), the choreographer Leonid Massine and the painter Pablo Picasso on the 1917 ballet *Parade* for Diaghilev's Ballets Russes. The work set out to introduce the principles of Cubism to the stage, and Satie's jazz-influenced score – including parts for typewriter, whistle and siren – caused a scandal. In complete contrast was the cantata *Socrate* (1919), which he wanted to be "white and pure like antiquity". Subsequent collaborations with Massine and Picasso, and with Francis Picabia and Réné Clair, produced the ballets *Mercure* and *Relâche (No Show,* 1924). By then Satie had become a recluse. A heavy drinker, he died of sclerosis of the liver in July 1925.

ABOVE: *An anonymous drawing of Satie in chalk, dated 1890 and inscribed "A mon ami Erik Satie" ("To my friend Erik Satie").*

Life and works

NATIONALITY: French

BORN: Honfleur, 1866;
DIED: Paris, 1925

SPECIALIST GENRES:
Minimalist piano music.

MAJOR WORKS:
Many piano works, including *Trois gymnopédies* (1888) and *Trois gnossiennes* (1890); ballet *Parade* (1917); cantata *Socrate* (1919).

Alexander Scriabin

It was like a bath of ice; cocaine and rainbows.

HENRY MILLER (1891–1980), "NEXUS"

Alexander Scriabin's early career has many parallels with Rachmaninov's. Like Rachmaninov, he was equally gifted as a composer and as a pianist. His mother (who died just over a year after he was born) had been a fine pianist, and he was brought up by female relatives.

Scriabin began his piano studies in Moscow with Nikolay Zverev – who also taught Rachmaninov – before entering the Conservatory in 1888, the same year as Rachmaninov. Shortly after graduating in 1892 with the second gold medal (Rachmaninov won the first), Scriabin came to the attention of the Russian millionaire publisher and philanthropist Belyayev, who began to publish his early works (including a set of 12 Studies), and sent him off on a European tour, playing his own music. From this period date several sets of piano Preludes, the Second Piano Sonata, and the Piano Concerto, which Scriabin composed on his return to Moscow.

In 1897 he married the young pianist Vera Isaakovich, with whom he had four children. But his intensely egotistical nature caused him to abandon her seven years later for another young admirer, his former pupil Tatiana Schloezer. At the same time, Scriabin gave up his teaching post at the Moscow Conservatory, and settled in Switzerland.

By 1903 he had already begun to compose orchestral music, including two symphonies, and was becoming increasingly involved in mysticism, dabbling in Nietzschean theories and

ABOVE: The Russian pianist and composer Alexander Scriabin (1872–1915), a portrait in oils by A.Y. Golovin.

the occult teachings of Madame Blavatsky, the founder of the Theosophical Society. Philosophical and mystical ideas began to influence his work from the Third Symphony (*Le divin poème*) onwards, particularly the sensuous *Poème de l'extase* (Poem of Ecstasy), and *Prométhée*, subtitled *Le poème du feu* (The Poem of Fire), in

which Scriabin developed the theory of synaesthesia, according to which art that appealed to all the senses would trigger a cataclysmic effect. To this end, different keys were associated with specific colours, demonstrated in performance by the use of coloured lighting. His Seventh and Ninth Piano Sonatas (1911 and 1912–13) are subtitled respectively *Messe blanche* and *Messe noire*.

In 1908 Scriabin returned to Russia, where his works were received with enormous enthusiasm. His later music, mostly for piano, is highly chromatic. In 1914 he visited London for a concert of his works conducted by Henry Wood, and during his stay he developed an ulcer on his lip which would not heal. He died of septicaemia on 27 April 1915.

Life and works

NATIONALITY: Russian

BORN: Moscow, 1872;
DIED: Moscow, 1915

SPECIALIST GENRES: Piano and orchestral music influenced by mysticism.

MAJOR WORKS: Ten sonatas and 85 preludes for piano; Piano Concerto (1896); *Le poème de l'extase* (1905–8); *Prométhée* (1910).

Ferruccio Busoni

I want to attain the unknown!

BUSONI, 1905

Like Scriabin, the pianist and composer Ferruccio Busoni was a maverick, important in his own right, but not profoundly influential. Italian by birth, he spent much of his career in Germany and Austria. His father was an Italian clarinettist, and his mother, a pianist of German origin. Busoni's parents began his musical education, and he gave his first public piano recital at the age of eight.

In 1876 the family moved to Graz, where Busoni conducted a performance of his own Stabat Mater (now lost), at the age of 12. He then moved to Vienna, where he met Brahms and dedicated to him the set of six Studies for piano, and an *Etude en forme de variation*. Brahms recommended that Busoni should move to Leipzig, where he met many eminent musicians, and wrote his Second String Quartet. He also began to make arrangements of

organ works by Bach, re-composing them in contemporary style.

In 1890 Busoni married the daughter of a Swedish sculptor, whom he had met in Helsinki (one of their sons

became a painter). He taught briefly in Moscow, but then decided to resume his career as a concert pianist in the USA. In 1894 he settled in Berlin, where he promoted orchestral concerts of the most avant-garde music, including works by Debussy, Bartók, Delius and Fauré.

Busoni also began to make daring harmonic experiments – similar to Schoenberg's although with a different approach – in his own music, especially in the set of Six Sonatinas for piano (1910–20). His orchestral music includes an extraordinary five-movement Piano Concerto which incorporates a male-voice chorus, and a more conventional Concertino for clarinet and chamber orchestra. Towards the end of his life he was preoccupied with stage works, including the operas *Die Brautwahl* (*The Bridal Choice*, after E. T. A. Hoffmann, 1912), and *Doktor Faust* (after Marlowe), which was left unfinished at his death.

ABOVE: The Italian/German composer Ferruccio Busoni (1866–1924).

LEFT: A scene from the 1999 Salzburg Festival production of Doktor Faust, Busoni's last opera, with Thomas Hampson as Faust and Chris Merritt as Mephistopheles.

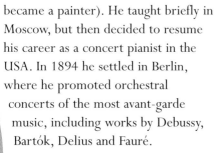

Life and works

NATIONALITY: Italian

BORN: Empoli, near Florence, 1866; **DIED:** Berlin, 1924

SPECIALIST GENRES: Virtuoso piano works, opera.

MAJOR WORKS: Piano Concerto (1904); *Arlecchino* (1914–16); *Doktor Faust* (1916–24).

Ralph Vaughan Williams

What we want in England is real music, even if it be only a music-hall song.

Vaughan Williams, "The Vocalist" (1902)

Vaughan Williams was one of a group of composers who contributed to the renaissance of English music in the 20th century. Born in Gloucestershire, he studied music at Cambridge University and the Royal College of Music, London, where his teachers included Parry and Stanford. (In later years, he also studied with Bruch and Ravel.) He began his career as a church organist in London and, with his friend Gustav Holst, initiated a systematic study and collection of English folk songs, which – together with his interest in Tudor music – profoundly influenced his own compositions.

In 1906 Vaughan Williams was appointed musical editor of *The English Hymnal*, for which he wrote some famous hymn tunes, such as "For All the Saints" (*Sine nomine*). He also became director of the amateur Leith Hill Music Festival in Dorking, Surrey, from 1905 until his death. From 1919 until 1939 he was a professor of composition at the Royal College of Music. He married twice, the first time in 1897; after his wife's death in 1951 he married the poet and librettist Ursula Wood.

Vaughan Williams' musical style has a distinctively "English" quality, derived from his use of the modality of folk song, tinged with an elusive mysticism. He was drawn to the mystical poetry of Walt Whitman, whose verses he set in *A Sea Symphony* (1903–9) and *Toward*

ABOVE: A photograph of Ralph Vaughan Williams (1872–1958), taken in 1952 – the year of his 80th birthday.

the Unknown Region (1905–6). Other early works included the *Fantasia on a Theme of Thomas Tallis* for double string orchestra and the settings of poems by A. E. Housman, *On Wenlock Edge* (1908), for voice and string quartet, as well as the ever-popular part-song "Linden Lea" (1901) and the *Songs of Travel* (1901–4), based on Robert Louis Stevenson's poems.

Altogether Vaughan Williams wrote nine symphonies, including No. 2 (*A London Symphony*, 1912–13), No. 3 (*Pastoral*, 1916–21), No. 5 (1938–43, which with the gritty No. 6 of 1944–7 was perceived as the composer's response to war), and the *Sinfonia*

antarctica (1949–52, based on his score for the 1948 film *Scott of the Antarctic*). His orchestral music also includes *The Lark Ascending* (a rhapsody for violin and orchestra), concertos for violin, oboe and tuba, *A Norfolk Rhapsody*, the Fantasia on "Greensleeves" (1934) and the overture *The Wasps* (1909).

Vaughan Williams wrote in many genres, including stage and film music. His six operas are relatively infrequently revived, but his ballet score *Job: A Masque for Dancing* has remained in the orchestral repertoire.

Life and works

NATIONALITY: English

BORN: Down Ampney, 1872; **DIED**: London, 1958

SPECIALIST GENRES: Symphonies, stage works influenced by English folk song.

MAJOR WORKS: Nine symphonies; *Fantasia on a Theme of Thomas Tallis* (1910); *The Lark Ascending* (1914); *Serenade to Music* (1938); operas *Hugh the Drover* (1910–14), *Sir John in Love* (1924–8), *Riders to the Sea* (1925–32) and *The Pilgrim's Progress* (1949); ballet *Job* (1927–30).

Gustav Holst

Never compose anything unless the not composing of it becomes a positive nuisance to you.

Holst was born into a less privileged background than his friend Vaughan Williams, whom he met as a fellow student at the Royal College of Music in London in the 1890s. His family was of Swedish descent, and his father was an organist and piano teacher in Cheltenham.

Holst earned a living first as a trombonist, and then as a teacher in London. From 1903–20 he taught music at a girls' school in Dulwich and in 1905 he was appointed director of music at St Paul's School for Girls in Hammersmith, where he remained until his death. He was also music director at Morley College, South London, from 1907–24, professor of music at Reading University, and a teacher at the Royal College of Music.

ABOVE: The British composer of Swedish origin Gustav Holst (1874–1934), photographed in 1925.

He lived in Richmond (where his daughter Imogen, who also became a composer, was born in 1907) and then had a riverside house in Barnes, but composed in his room in St Paul's School at weekends and during school holidays.

Like Vaughan Williams, Holst was strongly influenced by English folk song, which informed many of his works, including *A Somerset Rhapsody* (1906–7), the Suites for military band (1909–11), the *St Paul's* and *Brook Green* suites for strings (1913 and 1933), *A Moorside Suite* for brass band (1928) and the scherzo *Hammersmith* for military band or orchestra (1930–1).

Holst's interest in mysticism and Eastern religion also permeated his music. He learned Sanskrit in order to translate hymns from the Rig Veda,

which he set for chorus and orchestra in 1908; his first major work, *The Mystic Trumpeter*, was performed at the Queen's Hall in 1905, and oriental philosophy underpins his opera *Sāvitri*.

His most popular work is undoubtedly the orchestral suite *The Planets*, of which "Mars" is a terrifying vision of approaching war. The lyrical central section of "Jupiter" was later used to set the patriotic hymn "I Vow to Thee, My Country".

Towards the end of his life, Holst's style became more austere. His later works included the Hardy-inspired tone-poem *Egdon Heath* (1927), the Concerto for two violins (1929), the operas *At the Boar's Head* and *The Wandering Scholar* and the Choral Fantasia (1931). He died in 1934, following surgery for haemorrhagic gastritis.

ABOVE: The planets inspired Holst's most famous orchestral work.

Life and works

NATIONALITY: English

BORN: Cheltenham, 1874; **DIED:** London, 1934

SPECIALIST GENRES: Orchestral and stage works influenced by mysticism and native folk song.

MAJOR WORKS: *The Planets* (1914–16); operas *Sāvitri* (1908), *The Perfect Fool* (1922), *At the Boar's Head* (1924) and *The Wandering Scholar* (1929–30).

Frederick Delius

It is only that which cannot be expressed otherwise that is worth expressing in music.

DELIUS, "AT THE CROSSROADS" (1920)

A contemporary of Debussy, Delius was born in northern England but lived in France for much of his life. His musical style was an amalgam of English lyrical nostalgia, the Impressionism of Debussy, and Mahlerian post-Romanticism.

The son of a German-born wool merchant, Delius was brought up in Bradford, Yorkshire. His father attempted to dissuade him from considering a musical career and packed him off to Florida to manage an orange plantation, but while in America he studied music theory with an organist, Thomas Ward, and his father relented. In 1886 he was allowed to study music in Leipzig, where he befriended Grieg, but soon left to settle in Paris, where he became friends with the painters Paul Gauguin and Edvard Munch. From his Paris years date the operas *Irmelin* (1890) and *Koanga* (1895–7), the Piano Concerto (1897) and the tone-poem *Paris, the Song of a Great City* (1899).

In 1897 Delius married the Norwegian artist Jelka Rosen and settled in Grez-sur-Loing near Fontainebleau. However, his bohemian lifestyle in Paris had left him with the grim legacy of syphilis, which eventually killed him. His most famous opera, *A Village Romeo and Juliet* – a tragic *Tristan and Isolde*-like tale of young love doomed by parental emnity – was written between 1899 and 1901. From this period also date the distinctive works of his maturity, including *Brigg Fair* (1907, a set of variations on an English folk song), the cantata *Sea Drift* (a setting

ABOVE: Frederick Delius was born in Yorkshire but spent most of his life in France.

of Walt Whitman's poem), *A Mass of Life* (not a religious mass, but a setting of text from Nietzsche's *Also sprach Zarathustra*), the *Songs of Sunset* (1906–8), the First Dance Rhapsody for orchestra (1908) and the opera *Fennimore and Gerda* (1908–10).

Delius continued to compose prolifically through the second decade of the 20th century. The quintessentially "English"-sounding orchestral mood pictures *On Hearing the First Cuckoo in Spring* and *Summer Night on the River*, together with the *Song of the High Hills* for chorus and orchestra, date from 1911. During World War I he returned temporarily to England, where he wrote the Second Dance Rhapsody, sonatas for violin and cello, two concertos and his secular Requiem commemorating the war dead.

Although he spent very little of his life in England, his music still has a very "English", pastoral feel, enhanced by his fondness for triplet rhythmic patterns.

From 1922 onwards, as he became increasingly paralysed and his sight began to fail, he ceased to compose, but in 1928 he enlisted the help of the young Yorkshire musician Eric Fenby as his amanuensis. Among his later works are the *Songs of Farewell*, *A Song of Summer* for orchestra (1930), a third violin sonata, and the *Idyll* for soprano, baritone and orchestra (1930–2). He died at Grez in 1934, but was re-interred in Surrey a year later.

Life and works

NATIONALITY: English

BORN: Bradford, 1862;
DIED: Grez-sur-Loing, near Fontainebleau, 1934

SPECIALIST GENRES: Orchestral and choral music.

MAJOR WORKS: *A Village Romeo and Juliet* (1899–1901); *Appalachia* (1898–1903); *Sea Drift* (1903–4); *A Mass of Life* (1904–5); *Brigg Fair* (1907); Requiem (1914–16); Double Concerto (1915–16); Violin Concerto (1916); Cello Concerto (1921); *Songs of Farewell* (1930).

Leoš Janáček

I want to gather the sun's rays into my hands, I want to plunge myself in shadow,
I want to pour out my longings to the full: all directly.

JANÁČEK, 1927

Born in 1854, the Czech composer Leoš Janáček might have belonged to the late 19th-century nationalist tradition, the successor to Smetana, Dvořák and Suk. But in fact, most of his music dates from the last 30 years of his long life, and he is therefore regarded as a 20th-century composer. His reputation rests largely on the extraordinary series of late operas which, until the 1960s, were largely unknown outside Europe. The efforts of conductors such as Charles Mackerras brought them to the attention of British and American audiences, and they are now regarded as masterpieces.

Born in rural Moravia, the son of a schoolmaster, Janáček studied music in Brno, the capital of Moravia, and Prague. He then returned to Brno as a music teacher, founding an organ school there in 1881. The same year he married his pretty 15-year-old pupil, Zdenka Schulzová. Although the

ABOVE: *Leoš Janáček's work embodied the spirit of Czech nationalism, expressed in a moving and distinctive musical language.*

marriage was never formally dissolved, it was deeply unhappy almost from the start. The patriotic Janáček resented the fact that his wife was German-speaking, and they appear to have been sexually incompatible. Two children were born: their son Vladimir died at the age of two, and their daughter Olga at the age of 20, in 1903.

Folk songs

Janáček's early compositions include many choral pieces, for both mixed and male-voice choirs. While working on his first opera, *Šárka* (1887–8), he began to collect and edit Moravian folk songs, whose characteristic idioms – based on the flexible rhythms of speech – influenced his own compositions, giving them an entirely distinctive sound. His first important opera, *Jenůfa*, has a Moravian folk setting. This powerful tale of a young peasant girl's betrayal by her faithless lover, resulting in the murder of her newborn baby by her distraught foster-mother, was completed in 1903. It was first performed in Brno in January 1904, just before Janáček's 50th birthday.

LEFT: *Janáček with his young wife Zdenka Schulzová, photographed around the time of their ill-fated marriage.*

RIGHT: *Janáček's cottage at his birthplace, Hukvaldy. He was there with his great love Kamila Stösslová when he was taken fatally ill.*

Neither of his next two operas, *Osud* (*Fate*, 1903–7) and *Výlety páně Broučkovy* (*The Adventures of Mr Brouček*, 1908–18), based on a satirical novel by Svatopluk Čech, were notably successful. For the first two decades of the 20th century Janáček concentrated on piano music, notably the Sonata (1905), *Po zarostlém Chodníčku* (*On an Overgrown Path*, 1901–8) and *V mlhách* (*In the Mists*, 1912), chamber music and male-voice choruses. Up to this point he had written little orchestral music, but the tone-poem *Šumařovo dítě* (*The Fiddler's Child*) dates from 1912. *Taras Bulba*, an orchestral piece inspired by the heroic exploits of a Cossack leader, was written during World War I, and after the Czech Republic declared its independence in 1918, Janáček commemorated the event with *The Ballad of Blaník* (1920).

ABOVE: Costume design for the Vixen Bystrouška by Josef Capek (1887–1945) for the Prague première of The Cunning Little Vixen *on 18 May 1925.*

Late flowering

In May 1916 *Jenůfa* finally received its Prague première. Around the same time, the 62-year-old composer met Kamila Stösslová, the young wife of a Jewish antique-dealer. Despite the 38-year age gap between them, Janáček became infatuated with Kamila, and his passion for her inspired the radiant, life-affirming works of his old age. The first of these was *Zápisník zmizelého* (*The Diary of One who Disappeared*, 1917–19), a song-cycle dealing with a young man's love for a gypsy girl (Janáček constantly likened the dark-haired Kamila to a gypsy). This was followed by a stream of operas: the tragic *Katya Kabanová*, the life-enhancing *Příhody lišky bystroušky* (*The Cunning Little Vixen*), *Věc Makropulos* (*The Makropulos Case*), with its icy but fatally attractive heroine, and *Z mrtvého domu* (*From the House of the Dead*), based on Dostoyevsky's grim novel about life in a Siberian prison camp. Kamila appears in various guises in all these,

and she also inspired his two string quartets, *Kreutzer Sonata* (1923), based on Tolstoy's tale of adultery and revenge, and *Listy důvěrné* (*Intimate Letters*, 1928), as well as the wind sextet *Mládí* (*Youth*, 1924).

By now, Janáček was famous both at home and abroad. He visited England in 1926, shortly after writing the extrovert Sinfonietta, his best-known orchestral work. The same year he also completed the Glagolitic Mass, to an Orthodox text, and the Capriccio for piano (left hand) and chamber ensemble.

During the last seven years of his life, he worked mainly at his cottage at Hukvaldy, to which he often invited Kamila and her children. He was taken ill there in August 1928, and died in hospital of pneumonia. Kamila died seven years later; Janáček's wife, Zdenka, died in 1938.

ABOVE: A woman dressed in Moravian national costume, from the Brno area. Janáček loved to see Kamila wearing national dress.

Béla Bartók

*Bartók's name…stands for the principle and the demand for regeneration
stemming from the people, both in art and in politics.*

ZOLTÁN KODÁLY (1882–1967)

Bartók was the greatest Hungarian composer since Liszt. He and Kodály put Hungary on the international musical map.

Both Bartók's parents were musical, and he was taught the piano by his mother. He began to compose at the age of nine, and made his pianistic debut at 11. In 1903 he emerged from his studies at the Budapest Academy as a virtuoso pianist and a promising composer.

From the start, Bartók immersed himself in the idioms of Hungarian folk music. His first folk song collection was published in 1906, and in 1907 he became a piano professor at the Budapest Academy, a post which enabled him to pursue systematic research into folk music from Hungary, Romania, Slovakia and Transylvania. From this time onwards he began to publish folk song anthologies for voice and piano, and arrangements of

ABOVE: An evocative portrait by Roboz of the Hungarian pianist and composer Béla Bartók (1881–1945).

folk songs, such as *For Children* (1908–9). The Ten Easy Pieces, the 14 Bagatelles (both 1908) and the ferocious *Allegro barbaro* for piano (1911) are also strongly Hungarian in idiom. Another new influence, the atmospheric music of Debussy, informed Bartók's works from the First String Quartet (1908).

Works for the stage

In 1909 Bartók married his pupil Márta Ziegler, who gave birth to a son in 1910. The next year Bartók completed his one-act opera *A kékszakállú herceg vára* (*Duke Bluebeard's Castle*). This masterly score, based on a psychological interpretation of the Bluebeard legend, was not performed until 1918, after his ballet *A fából faragott királyfi* (*The Wooden Prince*) had been successfully staged in Budapest. Up to that point, Bartók's compositions had been largely neglected in his own country, but growing recognition of his talent prompted a second ballet, *A csodálatos mandarin* (*The Miraculous Mandarin*, 1918–19), whose sordid subject-matter caused outrage at its Cologne première in 1926. (The mandarin is lured into a robbers' den by a prostitute, but though stabbed and hanged by the men he refuses to die until he has had sex with her.)

During the post-war years Bartók began to tour widely as a pianist. In 1923 – when his Dance Suite, celebrating the 50th anniversary of the union of Buda and Pest, was premièred – he divorced Márta and married another young piano pupil, Ditta

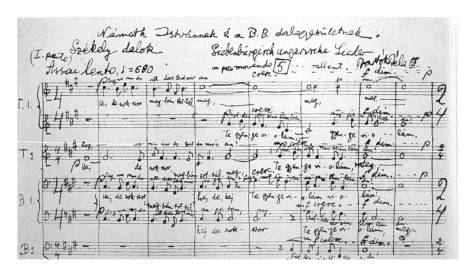

ABOVE: The opening manuscript page of Bartók's Hungarian folk song arrangements Székely dalok (Székely Songs) for six male voices (1932).

ABOVE: Bartók listening to his folk song recordings on a phonogram in 1915. He was one of the major folk song collectors.

ABOVE: Bartók giving a piano concerto performance in Budapest in 1938. His second wife, Ditta Pásztory, is sitting behind him.

Pásztory. A second son was born in 1924.

Meanwhile, Bartók continued his dual career as pianist and composer. Many of his piano works – such as the First and Second Concertos (1926 and 1930–1), the Sonata, the Suite *Out of Doors*, and the Nine Little Pieces (all 1926) – were written for himself to play. His Third and Fourth String Quartets date from the late 1920s, as do the two Rhapsodies for violin and piano, both written for Hungarian virtuosi. The *Cantata profana* (1930) – a paean to the brotherhood of nations – was premièred in London in 1934, the year Bartók finally relinquished his teaching duties at the Budapest Academy to concentrate on his ethnomusicological work.

New musical structures

The late '30s – a period during which Bartók was preoccupied with musical structure, especially arch forms and constructions based on mathematical rules – produced some of his finest compositions, including the Fifth and Sixth String Quartets. He was equally concerned with timbre, exploiting the innovative sounds produced on conventional instruments, in works such as the *Music for Strings, Percussion and Celesta* and the 1939 Divertimento for strings. The Sonata for two pianos and percussion (1937) was premièred by Bartók and his wife; the Second Violin Concerto (1937–8) was written for Zoltán Székely and *Contrasts* for the violinist Joseph Szigeti and the clarinettist Benny Goodman. During the 1930s Bartók also published *Microkosmos*, six books of piano teaching pieces.

America

In 1940, alarmed by the threat of fascism, the Bartóks left for America, where they settled in New York.

The last five years of Bartók's life were clouded by public neglect, financial worries and declining health. In 1943 he was diagnosed as suffering from a rare form of cancer. He completed his most popular work, the Concerto for Orchestra (premièred by Serge Koussevitsky and the Boston Symphony Orchestra), in the summer of 1943, and the solo Violin Sonata, written for Yehudi Menuhin, the following March. His last works were the Third Piano Concerto (1945), written for his wife, and the Viola Concerto for the Scottish-born player William Primrose, which was left unfinished at his death in September 1945.

ABOVE: The anti-hero of Duke Bluebeard's Castle, *portrayed by Janos Kass.*

Life and works

NATIONALITY: Hungarian

BORN: Nagyszentmiklos (now in Romania), 1881; **DIED:** New York, 1945

SPECIALIST GENRES: Orchestral and piano music influenced by central European folk idioms.

MAJOR WORKS: Six string quartets (1908–39); *Duke Bluebeard's Castle* (1911–18); *The Miraculous Mandarin* (1919); *Microkosmos* (1926–39); three piano concertos (1926–45); *Music for Strings, Percussion and Celesta* (1936); *Contrasts* (1938); Concerto for Orchestra (1943).

Zoltán Kodály

Some day the ringing tower of Hungarian music is going to stand.

KODÁLY, 1932

Like his friend and collaborator Bartók, Kodály raised the international profile of Hungarian music by fertilizing Western styles with Magyar folk idioms. An authority on folk music, he was also an important teacher, producing a vast body of musical educational material.

The son of a stationmaster, he spent his childhood and youth in the countryside, before enrolling at Budapest University to read languages. He simultaneously began to study composition at the Budapest Academy, where he was awarded a doctorate for his study of Hungarian folk song. From 1905 onwards he began to collect and record folk songs, often collaborating with Bartók, with whom he shared a vision of "an educated Hungary, reborn from the people". Like Bartók, Kodály devoted much of his life to the publication of folk song anthologies and arrangements.

ABOVE: Zoltán Kodály, photographed towards the end of his long life.

ABOVE: The Liszt Academy of Music in Budapest, where Kodály studied composition, and where he later became deputy director.

In 1906 he received a travelling scholarship to study in Berlin and Paris, where he came into contact with Debussy's music. On his return he was appointed a professor at the Budapest Academy, becoming its deputy director in 1919. But his tenure of that post was abruptly curtailed by political intrigue, and his career was only rescued after the triumphant 1923 première of his oratorio *Psalmus hungaricus*, written – like Bartók's Dance Suite – to celebrate the 50th anniversary of the union of Buda and Pest. A performance in Zurich in 1926 marked the beginning of his international fame.

The same year (1926), Kodály's opera *Háry János* was performed in Budapest, and world-famous conductors such as Arturo Toscanini, Rudolf Mengelberg and Wilhelm Furtwängler began to include the orchestral suite taken from it (which includes a prominent part for the cimbalom, a Hungarian dulcimer) in their repertoires. It was followed by other major orchestral works: the *Dances of Marosszek* (1930), the *Dances of Galánta* (1933), the *Peacock* Variations, based on a Hungarian folk tune (1939, written for the Amsterdam Concertgebouw Orchestra), and the Concerto for Orchestra (1939–40, for the Chicago Symphony). Like Bartók, Kodály opposed fascism, but he remained in Hungary when it came under Nazi rule. After the war he supervised the publication of the folk material he had collected, and continued to write educational works. In later life he was showered with honours.

Life and works

NATIONALITY: Hungarian

BORN: Kecskemét, 1882; **DIED:** Budapest, 1967

SPECIALIST GENRES: Orchestral and choral music influenced by folk music.

MAJOR WORKS: *Psalmus hungaricus* (1923); *Háry János* (1925–6); *Dances of Galánta* (1933); Concerto for Orchestra (1939–40).

Carl Nielsen

Music is life, and, like it, inextinguishable.

NIELSEN, MOTTO OF THE FOURTH SYMPHONY (1916)

Nielsen was the Danish equivalent of Grieg or Sibelius. Born into an impoverished family (his father was a painter), he began to scrape out melodies as a child on an instrument made from firewood. He started learning the violin at six and began playing in his father's folk band. In the mid 1880s he studied at the Copenhagen Conservatory, and first achieved success with his Little Suite for strings, performed at Tivoli in 1888.

The next year Nielsen became a violinist in the royal chapel, where he was able to broaden his musical outlook. During a trip to Paris in 1891 he met and married a sculptress, and on his return finished the first of a sequence of six symphonies, on which his reputation largely rests. No. 1 is an early example of "progressive tonality", beginning in one key and ending in another, while No. 2 (*The Four Temperaments*, 1901–2) uses the technique of thematic variation.

At much the same time Nielsen completed his first opera, *Saul og David*, followed a few years later by the comic opera *Maskarade*.

From 1908 until 1914 Nielsen combined composing with a position at the Royal Theatre, and then with teaching at the Copenhagen Conservatory, whose director he became in 1931, just before his death. He consolidated his foremost position in Danish musical life with three more symphonies (No. 3, *Sinfonia espansiva*, 1910–11; No. 4, *The Inextinguishable*, 1914–16; and No. 5, 1921–2), the Violin Concerto (1911), piano works including the Chaconne and the Theme and Variations, the tone-poem *Pan and Syrinx* (1917–18) and the exotic, colourfully scored incidental music to the play *Aladdin* (1918–19). His Fourth and Fifth Symphonies are imaginatively constructed, with innovative use of percussion (in a passage in the Fifth, the side-drum is instructed to improvise "in order to try to destroy the music").

Between 1914 and 1925 Nielsen published many volumes of Danish folk song arrangements, and his later works are mostly for chamber combinations or smaller orchestra. He died of heart disease in 1931.

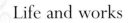

Life and works

NATIONALITY: Danish

BORN: Nørre-Lyndelse, near Odense, 1865; **DIED:** Copenhagen, 1931

SPECIALIST GENRES: Symphonies.

MAJOR WORKS: Six symphonies; *Saul og David* (1898–1901); *Maskarade* (1904–6).

ABOVE: The Danish composer Carl Nielsen (1865–1931), photographed as a young man.

RIGHT: The Royal Theatre in Copenhagen, where Nielsen's operas were performed, and where he worked from 1908–14.

Percy Grainger

I object to jazz and vaudeville having all the best instruments.

GRAINGER, 1930

The Australian composer and pianist Percy Grainger was brought up by his mother (to whom he was devoted) in Melbourne. In 1895 he left Australia for Europe, where he entered the Conservatory in Frankfurt; and in 1901 he settled in London to begin his career as a concert pianist, using it as a base for concert tours throughout Europe. He often visited Scandinavia, where he became a close friend of Grieg and a notable interpreter of his Piano Concerto; he was also a friend of Delius from 1907 onwards (Delius's orchestral rhapsody *Brigg Fair* is based on a Lincolnshire folk tune collected by Grainger).

In 1905 Grainger joined the English Folk Song Society, becoming an ardent folk song collector in company with

ABOVE: The Australian-born pianist and composer Percy Grainger (1882–1961).

Cecil Sharp, Holst and Vaughan Williams. Folk song infused much of his work, from piano arrangements such as the ever-popular *Country Gardens*, *Green Bushes*, *Molly on the Shore* and *Shepherds' Hey*, to arrangements for wind band, and original orchestral works such as *Mock Morris*. Much of his vocal music is now out of fashion, since he often set jingoistic verses by Kipling and other colonial writers. His original large-scale works, which include *The Warriors* for three pianos, orchestra and tuned percussion, have also fallen out of favour, with the exception of *Handel in the Strand* (1932) for strings, based

on Handel's *Harmonious Blacksmith* Variations treated in music-hall style.

In 1914 Grainger moved to the USA, where he became a US citizen, and settled in White Plains, New York State. His mother committed suicide in 1922, and over the next six years Grainger spent much time in Denmark, collecting Danish folk songs, and returned twice to Australia. In 1928 he married a Swedish artist, who was presumably willing to put up with his sado-masochistic sexual practices and other eccentricities – their wedding took place before a huge audience in the Hollywood Bowl. The rest of his life was a long creative decline, although he spent his last years experimenting with "free music", dispensing with the conventions of harmony, form and instrumentation.

ABOVE: Grainger at the piano with his adored (and domineering) mother, Rose, in the music room of their American home in 1921.

Life and works

NATIONALITY: Australian

BORN: Melbourne, 1882;
DIED: White Plains,
New York, 1961

SPECIALIST GENRES: Folk song settings and original works using ingenious instrumental combinations.

MAJOR WORKS: *The Warriors* (1912–16); *Handel in the Strand* (1932); Suite *A Lincolnshire Posy* (1940).

Charles Ives

This fascinating composer…was exploring the 1960s during the heyday of Strauss and Debussy.

IGOR STRAVINSKY (1882–1971)

Charles Ives, one of the most innovative figures in music history, was America's first major composer. His father was a town bandmaster with a most original musical mind. His experiments with acoustics and pitch, using quarter-tones, polytonality, tone clusters and simultaneously playing pieces in different keys, intrigued his young son. Ives later incorporated the unusual sounds of his childhood experiences into his own music.

In 1894 Charles went to Yale University, where he studied composition and wrote the first of his four symphonies. After graduating he moved to New York, where he worked in insurance, and by 1906 he and his partner, Julian Myrick, had set up their own very successful insurance agency

ABOVE: Charles Ives (1874–1954), an essentially amateur composer who gave American music an individual identity.

which made them millionaires. Ives married Harmony Twichell in a union of lasting happiness, but long hours of work combined with spare-time composing undermined his health, and in 1918 he had a heart attack. During a year's convalescence he embarked on the publication of his music. He retired from the insurance business in 1930.

Most of Ives's major compositions were written before 1920. Many were inspired by "American" landscapes, festivals, traditions, or historical events. They include four numbered symphonies (the Fourth introduces a chorus into the finale); the *Holidays Symphony* (1904–13), in which the movements are "Washington's Birthday", "Decoration Day", "Fourth of July" and "Thanksgiving Day"; *Central Park in the Dark* (1906); and three Sets for

orchestra, of which No. 1 is entitled *Three Places in New England*. He also wrote several psalm settings for various vocal combinations and organ or orchestra; over 20 Studies for piano, of which several describe stages of a baseball game; the huge *Concord* Sonata for piano, with optional parts for viola and flute; the epigrammatic three-page Sonata (1905) and the early *Variations on "America"* for organ.

Ives was a Satie-like figure, who often used punning titles (such as *Five Take-offs* or *Six Protests*). In *The Unanswered Question* (1906) for chamber ensemble, a solo trumpet asks "the question", to which a woodwind choir frantically attempts to find an answer. His innovative musical style had enormous influence on later American composers.

ABOVE: Yale University in New Haven, USA, where Ives studied in the 1890s. He was an enthusiastic member of the baseball team.

Life and works

NATIONALITY: American

BORN: Danbury, Connecticut, 1874; **DIED:** New York, 1954

SPECIALIST GENRES: Orchestral and piano music, often on American themes.

MAJOR WORKS: Five symphonies; *Variations on "America"* (1891); *Three Places in New England* (1904); Piano Sonata No. 2 *Concord* (1910–15); 114 songs.

Arnold Schoenberg

I am a conservative who was forced to become a revolutionary.

SCHOENBERG

Schoenberg was one of the seminal figures of 20th-century music. He loosened the grip of traditional tonality and explored new ways of working with the 12 notes of the chromatic scale. Although his own music is still generally misunderstood and has never achieved great popularity with audiences, his influence on other composers was immense.

He was born in Vienna, into an orthodox Jewish family, and began to learn the violin at eight. His father died when he was 15, and he was forced to leave school and take a job as a bank clerk. In the evenings he studied music, philosophy and literature, and taught himself to play the cello. His first composition lessons came from Alexander Zemlinsky, whose sister Mathilde he married in 1901. By that time he had written a string quartet, the string sextet *Verklärte Nacht* (*Transfigured Night*), and *Gurrelieder* (*Songs of Gurra*),

ABOVE: *The Austrian composer Arnold Schoenberg (1874–1951), painted by Richard Gerstl (1883–1908).*

for five voices, narrator, choir and orchestra. At that time Schoenberg was writing in a post-Romantic, Mahlerian style, but his works met with incomprehension from the start.

Berlin

At the end of 1901 Schoenberg moved to Berlin, where he supported his family (including his daughter Gertrud, born in 1902) first by providing and arranging music for a cabaret, and then by teaching at the Stern Conservatory.

He spent the next 30 years see-sawing between Berlin and Vienna, where he moved back in 1903 as a private teacher (his most notable pupils were Alban Berg and Anton Webern). His son Georg was born in Vienna in 1906.

By 1907–8 Schoenberg was experimenting with atonality and free dissonance, in works such as the First and Second Quartets, the song anthology *Das Buch der hängenden Gärten* (*The Book of the Hanging Gardens*), and the Three Piano Pieces, Op. 11, and in his major works of 1909 – the dramatic monologue *Erwartung* (*Awaiting*) and the Five Orchestral

ABOVE: *The Reichstag (Parliament) building in Berlin in Schoenberg's time. He moved to Berlin in 1901 and taught at the Stern Conservatory.*

ABOVE: *A drawing by B. F. Dolbin of Schoenberg directing a performance of his* Pierrot lunaire *on 17 November 1940.*

ABOVE: A view of modern-day Los Angeles. In 1936 Schoenberg was appointed Professor of Music at the University of Southern California, Los Angeles. He became an American citizen in 1941 and remained on the West Coast of the United States until his death in 1951, aged 76.

Pieces, Op. 16. They were greeted with outright hostility by the conservative Viennese, and when Schoenberg applied for a professorship at the Vienna Academy of Music and Dramatic Art, he encountered virulent anti-Semitism.

As a result, in 1911 he moved back to Berlin, where his *Pierrot lunaire* (*Moonstruck Pierrot*, 1912) for voice and chamber ensemble was well received. The work represents the first use of a technique Schoenberg called *Sprechstimme* ("speaking voice"), also known as *Sprechgesang* ("speech song"), in which the singer "speaks" rather than sings each note, starting on the pitch indicated but immediately leaving it in a rise or fall. Meanwhile, in 1912, the long-delayed orchestral version of *Gurrelieder* was applauded in Vienna, much to Schoenberg's disgust. Nonetheless he moved back to Vienna in 1915, when he briefly enlisted in the army but was discharged owing to poor health.

New tonality

After the war Schoenberg founded the Society for Private Musical Performances, which until 1921 gave some 350 performances of new music by himself, his pupils and colleagues. His works of the early 1920s laid the foundation of his revolutionary "12-note" style in the Five Piano Pieces, Op. 23, the Serenade and the Piano Suite. His wife died in 1923, but less than a year later he married Gertrud, sister of the violinist Rudolf Kolisch. He had three more children, including two sons born after he emigrated to the USA.

From 1925 until 1933 Schoenberg taught at the Prussian Academy of Arts in Berlin, where he wrote several major works including the Variations for Orchestra, and the operas *Von heute auf morgen* (*From One Day to the Next*, 1928–9) and *Moses und Aron* (1930–2; the title was deliberately spelt this way by Schoenberg to avoid the unlucky number of 13 letters). In 1933 Hitler's anti-Semitic legislation robbed him of his job and forced him to leave Germany for good, despite the fact that he had been baptized a Christian in 1898.

America

The family spent the summer in France, where Schoenberg re-converted to Judaism, and then sailed for America, where he began teaching in New York and Boston. A lifelong sufferer from asthma, he moved for the sake of his health to the West Coast, where he taught at the University of Southern California. His late works include concertos for violin and piano, the Fourth String Quartet (1936) and the String Trio (1946), the *Ode to Napoleon Buonaparte* (1942) and several pieces inspired by his faith, including *Kol nidre* (*All Vows*, 1938), his setting of the prayer for Yom Kippur, and *A Survivor from Warsaw* (1947). A deeply superstitious man, Schoenberg foretold his own death from heart failure on 13 July 1951.

Life and works

NATIONALITY: Austrian

BORN: Vienna, 1874;
DIED: Los Angeles, 1951

SPECIALIST GENRES:
Orchestral, chamber and piano music in styles varying from late Romantic to serialism.

MAJOR WORKS: *Verklärte Nacht* (1899); *Gurrelieder* (1900–11); Chamber Symphony No. 1 (1906); Three Piano Pieces, Op. 11 (1909); Five Orchestral Pieces, Op. 16 (1909); *Pierrot lunaire* (1912); Five Piano Pieces (1923); *Moses und Aron* (1930–51).

Alban Berg

The best music always results from ecstasies of logic.

BERG, IN "NEW YORK TIMES"

ABOVE: Alban Berg, the most accessible composer of the "Second Viennese School".

While Schoenberg's music is still an acquired taste, that of his pupil Alban Berg has always been more accessible to a wider audience. His two operas and his Violin Concerto are among the finest 20th-century works.

Like Webern, Berg spent most of his working life in Vienna, taking summer holidays in the Carinthian mountains where his family had an estate, and where he later bought a villa on the shores of Lake Wörther. He grew up surrounded by creative people – artists such as Gustav Klimt and Oskar Kokoschka, writers such as Peter Altenberg and Stefan Zweig – who formed a close-knit circle rather like the Schubertians of a century earlier. Around 1904 Berg began to study with Schoenberg: his first works include the beautiful Seven Early Songs (1905–8), which are clearly in the German Romantic tradition. But within a few years, by the time he wrote the Four Songs, Op. 2, Berg was already beginning to push traditional tonality to its limits, and the String Quartet, Op. 3 (1910), is a strikingly original piece, based around the whole-tone scale. The highly compressed *Altenberg-Lieder* of 1912 drew criticism from Schoenberg, who perhaps found them too original for his liking.

In 1911 Berg married Helene Nahowski after a four-year courtship. Until the 1970s their marriage was carefully portrayed (especially by the widowed Helene) as idyllically happy. But in 1977 a copy of the score of Berg's *Lyrische Suite* for string quartet (1925–6) came to light, heavily annotated by the composer, which left no doubt that this major work owed its existence to Berg's clandestine love-affair with a married woman, Hanna Fuchs-Robettin. The musical equivalents of her initials are interwoven with Berg's own to produce the underlying motif of the work.

LEFT: Adele Bloch-Bauer *by Gustav Klimt (1862–1918), an exponent of decadent, Symbolist art featuring* femmes fatales *like Berg's Lulu.*

ABOVE: A stage design by Vladislav Hofman for the last act of Berg's Wozzeck, *for the Prague première in 1926, one year after the opera's debut in Berlin.*

ABOVE: Wozzeck murders Marie in the last act of the 1990 English National Opera production of Wozzeck.

In September 1914 Berg sent Schoenberg two of his Three Orchestral Pieces, Op. 6, evidently hoping to heal the rift between them. Among Berg's most accessible orchestral works, the Three Pieces revert to a Mahlerian style, using traditional forms – "Prelude", "Round Dance" (with elements of Viennese dances, the waltz and the *Ländler*) and "March".

Operas

At the same time, Berg began work on the first of his two operas. He had seen the Viennese première of the 19th-century play *Wozzeck* by Georg Büchner (1813–37), and "at once decided to set it to music". But the war (during which he served in the Austrian army) intervened, and *Wozzeck* the opera was not completed until 1922, by which time Berg had had ample experience of the privations of a soldier's life at first hand.

Wozzeck is a masterpiece, both for its sympathetic portrayal of the main protagonists – the downtrodden, exploited soldier, and the faithless mistress whom he eventually murders – and for its complex, innovative structure. A carefully constructed sequence of scenes is grouped into three acts, with Acts I and III framing the pivotal central act; the five scenes in Act I are described as "character pieces", each relating Wozzeck to another character in the drama. Berg described Act II as a "symphony in five movements", focusing on Wozzeck's disintegrating relationship with Marie.

ABOVE: Manon Gropius, the daughter of Mahler's widow Alma and her second husband Walter Gropius.

Act III consists of five inventions, each based on an *ostinato* rhythmic pattern or theme. But Berg's genius ensured that the audience's attention is focused not on such compositional wizardry, but on the drama itself.

Similar structural complexities underpin his last opera, *Lulu*, based on Frank Wedekind's two plays *Erdgeist* (*Earth Spirit*) and *Die Büchse der Pandora* (*Pandora's Box*). Again, the drama pivots around the large-scale rondo structure of Act II, with Lulu's Act III clients (after her descent into prostitution) paralleling – dramatically and musically – her lovers in Act I. Her last, fatal, encounter is with Jack the Ripper.

Lulu remained incomplete at Berg's death, and there is evidence that his widow obstructed its completion and performance during her lifetime. Berg's work on the opera had been interrupted by the composition of his last completed work, the elegiac Violin Concerto, written as a Requiem for Manon Gropius (daughter of Mahler's widow Alma and her second husband, the architect Walter Gropius), who died at 18 from polio. Shortly after completing it in August 1935 Berg suffered an insect sting which turned septic. He died of septicaemia four months later, aged 50.

Anton Webern

He shook the foundation of sound as discourse in favour of sound as sound.

JOHN CAGE (1912–92)

Webern produced perhaps the most compressed output of any composer in history: his complete works – some of which last only a few seconds in performance – have been recorded on to three CDs. He adopted the serial (12-note) technique of his teacher Schoenberg, and pursued it with ruthless concentration, paring it down to its essence.

Webern grew up in Vienna, Graz and Klagenfurt (his aristocratic family had a summer estate in Carinthia, where he developed a life-long love of walking, botany and geology). He was taught the piano by his mother, and after leaving school in 1902 he went to the University of Vienna, where he studied musicology,

ABOVE: Anton Webern (1883–1945), a composer of extreme intellectual rigour.

composition, cello and piano. His early works, including the Piano Quintet (1907) and the Op. 1 Passacaglia for orchestra (1908), are in the Brahmsian tradition.

Between 1904 and 1908 Webern studied privately with Schoenberg. From 1908 onwards he held various conducting posts, and played a leading role in the Society for Private Musical Performances, for which he made many chamber arrangements of pieces by himself and others. In the 1920s and early '30s he conducted many workers' choral societies and symphony concerts, at which he introduced works by Mahler, his fellow pupil Berg, Max Reger and even Charles Ives. From 1927 he was employed as music adviser to Austrian

Radio, but he lost all these jobs under the Nazi regime, when his music was banned. From 1938 onwards he worked as a freelance for his publisher, Universal Edition. He was accidentally shot dead by an American soldier during the last weeks of World War II, while visiting his daughter.

Webern's works up to the late 1920s were atonal in style. From 1928 onwards he adopted serial technique, often using *Klangfarbenmelodie* (timbre melody), in which changes of timbre rather than pitch define the melody. Many of his works are scored for chamber ensembles and use complex structural forms such as canon, palindrome and variation form.

ABOVE: Anton Webern at the keyboard.

Life and works

NATIONALITY: Austrian

BORN: Vienna, 1883; **DIED:** Mittersill, near Salzburg, 1945

SPECIALIST GENRES: Chamber and orchestral works.

MAJOR WORKS: Symphony, Op. 21 (1928); Concerto for nine instruments, Op. 24 (1931–4); three cantatas; String Quartet, Op. 28 (1936–8); piano Variations (1935–6); orchestral Variations (1940).

Kurt Weill

I write for today. I don't care about posterity.

WEILL

Kurt Weill was the musical personification of the Weimar Republic. His acidic blend of social realism and jazz reflected the decadent Germany of the 1920s, a time of economic depression, political upheaval and desperate hedonism. Together with his principal collaborator Bertolt Brecht (1898–1956), Weill created a new genre of music theatre, which he later developed on Broadway after his emigration to the USA.

The son of a Jewish cantor in Dessau, Weill studied briefly at the Berlin Hochschule and took masterclasses with Busoni. His first major work, the opera *Der Protagonist*, was performed in Dresden in 1926, and shortly afterwards he was introduced to the left-wing playwright Bertolt Brecht. Among the first fruits

ABOVE: Kurt Weill (1900–50), photographed after his move to the USA.

of the Brecht/Weill collaboration was *Die Dreigroschenoper* (*The Threepenny Opera*), a modern reworking of John Gay's *The Beggar's Opera* (1728), an English ballad opera set in the Soho underworld of thieves and pimps. It was premièred in Berlin in 1928 (with Weill's wife, Lotte Lenya, as Jenny), and scored a huge success with its bitter-sweet jazz idioms and savagely ironic subject. Its central song, "The Ballad of Mack the Knife", became an international hit.

In 1930 the partnership's second opera – *Aufstieg und Fall der Stadt Mahagonny* (*The Rise and Fall of the City of Mahagonny*) – was premièred in Leipzig. By now Weill's music had

been targeted by the emerging forces of fascism, and after the Nazi seizure of power in 1933 Weill fled to France, where his ballet *Die sieben Todesünden* (*The Seven Deadly Sins*), to a scenario by Brecht, was produced in Paris without much success.

In 1935 Weill left France for the USA, where he settled permanently. In 1938 he achieved his first Broadway success with *Knickerbocker Holiday*, which contains the evocative "September Song". He went on to write another ten Broadway shows, of which the best known are *Lady in the Dark* (with Ira Gershwin, 1940), *One Touch of Venus* (1943), *Street Scene* (1946), and *Lost in the Stars* (1949). He also wrote film and radio scores, but all his concert music, which includes a Violin Concerto (1924) and two symphonies, belongs to his "German" period.

ABOVE: An album of songs from Weill's famous work, The Threepenny Opera *(1928).*

Life and works

NATIONALITY: German

BORN: Dessau, 1900;
DIED: New York, 1950

SPECIALIST GENRES:
Theatre music using jazz and cabaret idioms.

MAJOR WORKS:
Die Dreigroschenoper (1928); *Aufstieg und Fall der Stadt Mahagonny* (1930).

Francis Poulenc and "Les Six"

Above all do not analyse my music – love it!

POULENC

"Les Six" was the appellation given in 1920 by the French critic Henri Collet to a group of promising young avant-garde composers, who specialized in "shocking the bourgeoisie" along the lines of their mentor, Erik Satie. As a homogeneous group, Les Six – who drew their inspiration from Parisian streetlife, music halls and circus bands – lasted only a few years before going their separate ways.

The most important member was Francis Poulenc, who first attracted attention with his *Rapsodie nègre* for baritone and chamber ensemble (1917). Born into the family of pharmaceutical manufacturers which is now the multinational Rhône-Poulenc company, Poulenc never had to earn a living. He began learning the piano at five, and later studied with the Spanish pianist Ricardo Viñes (1875–1943). In the early 1920s he took private composition lessons, his first major work being settings of Cocteau's *Cocardes*

(1919). Stravinsky recommended Poulenc to the impresario Sergei Diaghilev, who commissioned the ballet with chorus *Les biches* (1923). A sophisticated blend of lyricism with 1920s jazz idioms, the ballet was a great success, but during the 1920s and early '30s Poulenc concentrated on songs – many written for his recital partner, the baritone Pierre Bernac

(1899–1979) – and piano music, including two chamber concertos.

He might have remained an essentially frivolous composer, had not the death of a close friend in a car crash prompted his re-conversion to Catholicism. Poulenc visited the shrine of the Black Virgin at Rocamadour, and the musical result – *Litanies à la vierge noire* (1936) – was the first of a series of fine sacred works. These included the Mass in G (1937), two motets for unaccompanied choir (1941), the Stabat Mater (1950) and the exultant Gloria (1959).

Other important late works include the Sextet and sonatas for cello, violin, flute, clarinet and oboe; the operas *Les mamelles de Tirésias* (*The Breasts of Tirésias*), *Les dialogues des Carmélites*

ABOVE:
Francis Poulenc
(1899–1963),
photographed
in 1949.

LEFT: Parisians
enjoying
themselves in the
1920s –
Dancing at the
Moulin Rouge
by Marcel Leprin
(1891–1933).

Life and works

NATIONALITY: French

BORN: Paris, 1899;
DIED: Paris, 1963

SPECIALIST GENRES: Stage works, concertos, piano music, sacred vocal music.

MAJOR WORKS: Concerto in D minor for two pianos (1932); Organ Concerto (1938); *Les mamelles de Tirésias* (1944); Stabat Mater (1950); *Les dialogues des Carmélites* (1953–6); *La voix humaine* (1958); Gloria (1959).

(the story of a group of nuns during the French Revolution) and *La voix humaine* (*The Human Voice*), the cantata *Figure humaine* (1943), and concertos for organ and piano. All these works allowed Poulenc to develop a naturally lyrical style leavened with wit and irony.

Arthur Honegger

The Swiss composer Honegger (1892–1955) came to fame first with his "dramatic psalm" *Le roi David* (1921), and again three years later with *Pacific 231*, a musical representation of a steam locomotive. A great admirer of Bach, whose influence is evident in his music, Honegger's best-known works are his five symphonies, particularly No. 3, *Liturgique* (1945–6), No. 4, *Deliciae basilienses* (1946), and No. 5, *Di tre re* (*Of the three Ds*, 1950); the *Pastorale d'été* (*Summer Pastoral*, 1920); and the staged oratorio *Jeanne d'Arc au bûcher* (*Joan of Arc at the Stake*, 1934–5), based on a text by Paul Claudel.

ABOVE: Five of "Les Six" with the poet Jean Cocteau, on the viewing platform of the Eiffel Tower in 1921. From left to right: Tailleferre, Poulenc, Honegger, Milhaud, Cocteau and Auric.

Darius Milhaud

Milhaud (1892–1974) studied at the Paris Conservatoire, where he later taught after World War II. The only Jewish member of Les Six, he was forced to leave France in 1940 and settled in the USA, where he taught in California and Colorado. Milhaud (who spent much of his life in a wheelchair due to rheumatoid arthritis) experimented with polytonality. An enormously prolific composer, he is best known for his 1919 jazz and Latin American-influenced ballet score *Le boeuf sur le toit* (*The Ox on the Roof*); the ballet *La création du monde* (1923); and

for the two-piano suite *Scaramouche* (1939). Many of his stage works were based on his friend the poet Paul Claudel's adaptations of Greek myths.

Other members of Les Six

Of the three less well-known members of Les Six, Georges Auric (1899–1983) began as a composer for Diaghilev's Ballets Russes in the 1920s and went on to specialize in film music, writing the scores for the films of Jean Cocteau.

Louis Durey (1888–1979) was only briefly a member of the group. In 1936 he joined the French Communist Party, and after 1945 wrote "music for the masses" in accordance with communist doctrine, setting texts by Mao Zedong and Ho Chi-Minh.

Germaine Tailleferre (1892–1983) was a fine pianist, who wrote over a dozen operas, two ballets, orchestral music including concertos for piano and harp, chamber music including a Pastorale for flute and piano and two violin sonatas, songs, and a few piano pieces. However, her two husbands apparently both discouraged her from composing.

ABOVE: Arthur Honegger (1892–1955).

ABOVE: The French composer Darius Milhaud (1892–1974) conducting.

Aaron Copland

*Music that is born complex is not inherently better or worse
than music that is born simple.*

COPLAND

Copland was the most influential American composer of his time. He strove to create a recognizable "American" idiom, and came to represent the "Establishment" in American music, even though he himself was an outsider, by virtue both of his immigrant background and his homosexuality. Although his life spanned almost the whole of the 20th century, many of his most important works date from the first half of the century.

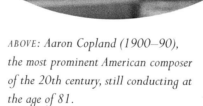

ABOVE: *Aaron Copland (1900–90), the most prominent American composer of the 20th century, still conducting at the age of 81.*

Copland's parents were Lithuanian/ Russian Jews who had become prosperous Brooklyn storekeepers, and he grew up with a keen interest in music. From 1917 he took composition lessons with the conservative Rubin Goldmark in New York, but when he was 20 he decided to seek more creative stimulation in Paris.

He studied for four years with Nadia Boulanger (1887–1979), one of the most dynamic teachers of her age, and threw himself into the frenzied creative melting-pot of 1920s Paris, absorbing influences from all directions, including Stravinsky and Les Six. In 1925 his Organ Symphony (which he

revised in 1928, without organ, as Symphony No. 1) was performed by Nadia Boulanger on an American tour, eliciting the admiring comment from the conductor Walter Damrosch (1862–1950): "If he can write like that at 23, in five years he'll be ready to commit murder." On his return to New York, Copland divided his time between teaching and composing, joining the League of Composers and – with his fellow composer Roger Sessions (1896–1985) – sponsoring an innovative series of new music concerts in New York.

ABOVE: *Eugene Loring as Billy in the original Ballet Caravan production of Copland's* Billy the Kid *at the Chicago Opera House, 16 October 1938.*

Life and works

NATIONALITY: American

BORN: New York, 1900;
DIED: New York, 1990

SPECIALIST GENRES:
"American" ballet scores, orchestral music.

MAJOR WORKS:
Piano Concerto (1926); *Billy the Kid* (1938); *Fanfare for the Common Man* (1942); *Rodeo* (1942); *Appalachian Spring* (1944); Symphony No. 3 (1944–6).

Popular music

Copland had firm convictions about the role of music in society, and was determined to show that the arts and industry could co-exist on equal terms. His ideas were honed by the Depression and the looming war: he decided that his own music must be, above all, accessible, and he gave it a specifically American sound by incorporating elements of jazz and folk music. Copland's first major hit was the ballet *El salón México* (1936), and from 1938 onwards he produced a series of influential ballets on "American" subjects: *Billy the Kid*, *Rodeo* (for Agnes de Mille) and *Appalachian Spring*. This last, written for Martha Graham's dance company, is a tender portrait of a close-knit pioneering community in the Appalachian mountains, whose aspirations are embodied in the Shaker hymn-tune "Simple Gifts". At the same time he began to write film scores, of which the best-known were for *Of Mice and Men* (1939), *Our Town* (1940), *The Red Pony* (1948) and the Oscar-winning *The Heiress* (1949).

Several other notable works date from this specifically "American" period, including the urban landscape *Quiet City* (1939), *A Lincoln Portrait* for speaker and orchestra (1942), based on Lincoln's speeches; and *Fanfare for the*

ABOVE: A steer wrestler in action at a rodeo in Idaho. Copland's "cowboy ballet" Rodeo *celebrates this American tradition.*

Common Man, written as an antidote to the usual pompous VIP fanfares. His Piano Variations of 1930 remains his best-known solo work (a Piano Sonata dates from 1939–41, and a Violin Sonata from 1943).

Serialism

Copland's post-war works were more abstract and notably less successful: by then fashions were changing and the fast-paced modern idioms of Leonard Bernstein had overtaken Copland's in the popularity stakes. Among his later works, the beautiful *Twelve Poems of*

Emily Dickinson for voice and piano (1950), the Piano Quartet (1950, which uses 12-note technique), the orchestral *Music for a Great City* (1964), and the *Threnody in memoriam Stravinsky* for flute quartet (1971) are the most memorable. His opera *The Tender Land* (1952–4) was not well received.

From 1940–65 Copland was head of the composition faculty at the Berkshire Music Center at Tanglewood, and also taught at Harvard, where his lectures were published as *Music and Imagination* (1952). He was showered with honours, including a Pulitzer Prize.

ABOVE: A pastoral landscape in the Appalachians, such as inspired Copland's ballet Appalachian Spring *(1944).*

ABOVE: Martha Graham in Appalachian Spring, *seen here with her dance company in 1954.*

George Gershwin

I don't think there has been such an inspired melodist on this earth since Tchaikovsky...
but if you want to speak of a composer, that's another matter.

LEONARD BERNSTEIN (1918–90)

Gershwin was one of the most popular composers of the 20th century, and one of history's greatest songwriters. From 1916 until his untimely death from a brain tumour at the age of only 39, he turned out a stream of great melodies which became instant classics. Songs such as "Swanee", "'S Wonderful", "Someone to Watch Over Me", "Embraceable You", "He Loves and She Loves", "I Got Rhythm" (and dozens more) rank with the best of Irving Berlin, Cole Porter and Jerome Kern, but were also much admired by "serious" musicians.

The son of a Russian Jewish immigrant family, Gershwin studied piano, theory and harmony as a child with several distinguished musicians, although he was never good at reading music. In 1914 he went to work for a Tin Pan Alley music publisher and began to write songs for other people's shows. From 1919 onwards he wrote his own Broadway musicals, many in collaboration with his brother Ira

(1896–1983). They included *Lady be Good* (1924), *Oh, Kay!* (1926), *Strike Up the Band* (1927), *Funny Face* (1927), *Girl Crazy* (1930) and *Of Thee I Sing* (1931). From 1931 onwards he also wrote film scores (the songs "Let's Call the Whole Thing Off", "Shall We Dance?" and "They Can't Take That Away From Me"

were written for the 1937 film *Shall We Dance?*).

In 1924 the bandleader Paul Whiteman commissioned Gershwin's famous *Rhapsody in Blue* for piano and jazz ensemble. The story goes that Gershwin did not know he was supposed to write it until he saw an advertisement for Whiteman's forthcoming "Experiment in Modern Music" concert in a newspaper. Ira Gershwin suggested the title, after a painting by Whistler. Its triumphant success led to commissions for the Piano Concerto, the orchestral tone-poem *An American in Paris*, and ultimately to the opera *Porgy and Bess*, set among the black community of the Deep South and using its folk music and rhythms. It is still the only American opera to be performed internationally on a regular basis.

ABOVE: George Gershwin, painted by himself a year before his death from a brain tumour.

LEFT: A poster advertising the 1959 film version of Porgy and Bess.

Life and works

NATIONALITY: American

BORN: Brooklyn, 1898;
DIED: Beverly Hills, 1937

SPECIALIST GENRES: Popular songs.

MAJOR WORKS: *Rhapsody in Blue* (1924); Piano Concerto in F (1925); Preludes for piano (1926); *An American in Paris* (1928); *Porgy and Bess* (1935).

Samuel Barber

*As to what happens when I compose,
I really haven't the faintest idea.*

BARBER

Samuel Barber's style eschewed the idiomatic "Americanisms" of Copland and looked back to the late-Romantic European tradition. He began to learn the piano at the age of six, and began composing at seven. At 14 he became one of the first students at the Curtis Institute in Philadelphia, where he studied piano, composition, conducting and singing. He nearly became a professional baritone.

Barber's student years at the Curtis Institute produced his first mature compositions, including the popular *Dover Beach* (a setting of a poem by Matthew Arnold for baritone voice and string quartet which Barber himself recorded in 1935), the Serenade for string quartet, and the

ABOVE: The American composer Samuel Barber (1910–81).

Cello Sonata, all of which gave him scope to develop his characteristic lyrical, expressive style. In 1928 he won a travelling scholarship with his Violin Sonata, and another in 1933 for his overture *The School for Scandal*. In the mid 1930s further scholarships, including the American Prix de Rome, enabled him to spend time in Italy. His compositions there included the First Symphony and a String Quartet, the slow movement of which, transcribed for orchestra, became the famous Adagio for strings (first recorded by Toscanini).

From 1939 until 1942 Barber taught at the Curtis Institute, and from 1943

until 1974 he lived in New York State with the Italian composer Gian Carlo Menotti (born 1911), who wrote the libretto for Barber's first opera, *Vanessa*. His Second Symphony (later withdrawn) was written during war service. His post-war works included a fine Cello Concerto (1945), the ballet *Medea* (1946), the Piano Sonata, *Summer Music* for wind quintet (1955), the vocal works *Knoxville: Summer of 1915* (1947), *Hermit Songs* (1952–3), and *Prayers of Kierkegaard* (1954), and three operas, of which *Antony and Cleopatra* (1965–6), based on Franco Zeffirelli's reworking of Shakespeare, was an expensive failure. A post-Romantic, Barber shunned innovation, and continued, as he said, to "go on doing his thing" until the end of his life.

Life and works

NATIONALITY: American

BORN: West Chester, Pennsylvania, 1910; **DIED:** New York, 1981

SPECIALIST GENRES: Orchestral, chamber and operatic works, in neo-Romantic idiom.

MAJOR WORKS: *Dover Beach* (1931); *The School for Scandal* Overture (1933); Adagio for strings (1938); Piano Sonata (1949); opera *Vanessa* (1958); Piano Concerto (1962).

ABOVE: Philadelphia, Pennsylvania, at dusk. Barber studied there at the world-famous Curtis Institute.

Igor Stravinsky

Bach on the wrong notes.

SERGEI PROKOFIEV (1891–1953)

Stravinsky was arguably the greatest – and certainly the most versatile – composer of the 20th century. He was keenly receptive to new trends – from neo-classicism to 12-note music – and perceived the advantages of a protean approach to composition. He also shed his personal skin several times throughout his long life, acquiring two wives and three changes of nationality.

Russian period

The son of an opera singer, Stravinsky went to school in St Petersburg, and began piano lessons when he was nine. On a summer vacation in the country he met Rimsky-Korsakov, who became his teacher and mentor. His early Piano Sonata in F sharp minor was performed at Rimsky-Korsakov's house, and a Symphony in E flat and the orchestral fantasy *Feu d'artifice* (*Fireworks*, strongly influenced

ABOVE: *Igor Stravinsky, photographed by Tappe in 1965, while he was writing the* Requiem Canticles, *his last major work.*

by Debussy) were largely written under the elder composer's tuition. Stravinsky had no other formal musical education; during this time he spent a couple of years reading law at university, but found it uncongenial. He left in 1905 and the following year he married his cousin Katerina Nossenko, who bore him four children.

Diaghilev's Ballets Russes

In 1909 the *Scherzo fantastique* and *Feu d'artifice* were performed in St Petersburg. In the audience was the impresario Sergei Diaghilev (1872–1929), whose celebrated Ballets Russes employed the dancer Mikhail Fokine and the designers Léon Bakst and Alexandre Benois. Diaghilev lacked a composer for his 1910 Paris season, and he decided to try out the young Stravinsky with a commission for *L'oiseau de feu* (*The Firebird*), based on a Russian folk legend. Stravinsky's brilliant and colourful score – strongly influenced by his Russian forebears including Balakirev, Tchaikovsky and Rimsky-Korsakov – was a huge success.

His next score for Diaghilev began life as a concert piece for piano and orchestra, but then turned into *Petrushka*, based on a grotesque tale of lust and murder in a Russian puppeteer's booth. Another huge success at its Paris première in June 1911, *Petrushka* conjures up a vanishing world of Russian peasant life, complete

ABOVE: *A portrait of Stravinsky conducting, by the artist Milein Cosman. Stravinsky conducted recordings of his entire output.*

with exotic and exhilarating dances for Cossacks, coachmen, wet-nurses and a host of other characters.

During 1912 Stravinsky worked on his third Diaghilev ballet, *Le sacre du printemps* (*The Rite of Spring*). Its première at the Théâtre des Champs-Elysées on 29 May 1913 caused a riot among its outraged audience. Even now, the primitive violence of Stravinsky's score – especially when coupled with Nijinsky's explicit choreography (the ballet concerns an ancient fertility rite in which a young virgin is selected for ritual sacrifice) – still packs an electrifying punch.

In 1914 Stravinsky's first opera, *Le rossignol* (*The Nightingale*, based on Hans Christian Andersen's fairy-story), was produced under the aegis of the Ballets Russes at the Paris Opéra. (Five years later Stravinsky arranged the music as a symphonic poem, *Le chant du rossignol*, which was choreographed

ABOVE: *Stravinsky in his study in later life – a photographic portrait by Karsh of Ottawa.*

as a ballet by Leonid Massine with designs by Henri Matisse.)

When war broke out the composer and his family took refuge in Switzerland, where he worked on a new ballet score, *Les noces* (*The Wedding*), scored for four-part chorus,

four soloists, four pianos and percussion ensemble. Stravinsky's researches into Russian folk music for this project also inspired several secondary works, including the burlesque *Renard* (1915–16).

By 1918 Stravinsky had already abandoned the lush orchestral resources of his pre-war ballets in favour of more sparsely scored, chamber-orientated works. These included *L'histoire du soldat* (*The Soldier's Tale*, for three actors, dancer, and small instrumental ensemble) and the ballet *Pulcinella*, based on a *commedia dell'arte* theme with music "arranged" from fragments attributed to Pergolesi, at the suggestion of Diaghilev. *Pulcinella* – which ushered in Stravinsky's absorption in neo-classicism – was first performed at the Paris Opéra on 15 May 1920, with décor and costumes by Picasso. Stravinsky later arranged the music as suites for cello and piano and for violin and piano.

ABOVE: *The Moor, the Ballerina and Petrushka – a 1913 illustration by René Bull of the three main characters in Stravinsky's ballet* Petrushka.

Life and works

NATIONALITY: Russian

BORN: Oranienbaum, near St Petersburg, 1882; DIED: New York, 1971

SPECIALIST GENRES: Stage works (ballet, opera, oratorios), sacred music.

MAJOR WORKS: *L'oiseau de feu* (1910); *Petrushka* (1911); *Le sacre du printemps* (1912); *L'histoire du soldat* (1918); *Les noces* (1914–23); *Oedipus rex* (1926–7); *Symphony of Psalms* (1930); *Dumbarton Oaks* (1938); Symphony in Three Movements (1942–5); *The Rake's Progress* (1948–51).

ABOVE: *Cynthia Harvey and Anthony Dowell as the Firebird and the Prince in the Royal Ballet's production of* The Firebird, *Stravinsky's first ballet score for Diaghilev.*

ABOVE: *A scene from Stravinsky's third Diaghilev ballet,* The Rite of Spring.

French period

After the war, Stravinsky decided to make France his home, settling in Paris and Biarritz. The early 1920s saw the composition of several purely instrumental works, including the *Symphonies of Wind Instruments* (1921), dedicated to Debussy's memory, and the Concerto for Piano and Wind (1923–4). He also worked on *Mavra*: a one-act *opera buffa* based on Pushkin, and completed the orchestration of *Les noces*. These two works marked the end of his "Russian" period. At the same time, he began an affair with a married actress, Vera Soudeikine, to whom he dedicated the Octet for wind instruments (1922–3). To his wife Katarina he dedicated the Serenade in A (1925), one of many piano works written in the 1920s which also included the Capriccio for piano and orchestra (1928–9) and the Sonata (1924).

In 1927 Stravinsky celebrated the 20th anniversary of Diaghilev's first Paris season with the opera-oratorio *Oedipus rex*, based on a Latin version of the tragic myth by the poet Jean Cocteau. Neither Diaghilev nor the audience really appreciated this strange hybrid, which is now recognized as a masterpiece. Stravinsky had already begun to cut loose from Diaghilev. His next ballet score, *Apollon musagète* (a title later abbreviated to *Apollo*), was written to a commission from the American patroness Elizabeth Sprague Coolidge, and was the first of Stravinsky's ballets to be choreographed by George Balanchine (1904–83). It was followed by *Le baiser de la fée* (*The Fairy's Kiss*), a Tchaikovskian pastiche, for Ida Rubinstein's rival troupe. Diaghilev had little time to complain: he died in Venice in August 1929. The following year, Stravinsky was commissioned by Serge Koussevitzsky (1876–1951) to celebrate the 50th anniversary of the Boston Symphony Orchestra with the *Symphony of Psalms*; and in 1931 he began an association with the violinist Samuel Dushkin, for whom he wrote the Violin Concerto and the Duo Concertante for violin and piano.

In 1934 Stravinsky became a naturalized French citizen. The same year he collaborated with André Gide

ABOVE: *Stravinsky (right), photographed in 1921 with the impresario Sergei Diaghilev, founder of the Ballets Russes.*

ABOVE: *Stravinsky conducting in later life. He moved to the USA in 1939 and remained there for the rest of his life.*

ABOVE: Stravinsky rehearsing the orchestra of La Scala, Milan, in preparation for the première of his opera The Rake's Progress.

(1869–1951) on the musical melodrama *Perséphone*, again for Rubinstein, which was coolly received. But by the mid 1930s his main commissions were coming from the other side of the Atlantic. They included the ballet *Jeu de cartes* (*The Card Game*, choreographed by Balanchine in 1937 for the American Ballet), the pseudo-Baroque chamber concerto *Dumbarton Oaks*, and the Symphony in C for the Chicago Symphony Orchestra (1940).

American period

The imminent outbreak of World War II, combined with the deaths of his elder daughter, his wife and his mother, drove Stravinsky to seek sanctuary in the USA. On 9 March 1940 he married Vera Soudeikine, then settled in Hollywood and applied for US citizenship. The early works of his American years include the Symphony in Three Movements, the *Circus Polka* (1942) for dancing elephants in the Barnum and Bailey Circus, *Scènes de ballet* (1944) for a Broadway revue, the *Danses concertantes* (1941–2), and the *Ebony Concerto* for the jazz clarinettist

Woody Herman (1913–87). Stravinsky's last neo-classical work was the opera *The Rake's Progress* (1948–51), inspired by William Hogarth's famous series of etchings, to a libretto by W. H. Auden (1907–73) and Chester Kallman (1921–75). It was premièred in Venice in September 1951.

Last works

After *The Rake's Progress* Stravinsky's style underwent a major change. His meeting in 1948 with the conductor Robert Craft (born 1923), an admirer of Schoenberg, introduced Stravinsky to the music of the Second Viennese School. The first fruit of his own experiments with serial technique was the *Canticum sacrum* (1955), designed for performance in St Mark's, Venice. Two further stage works date from his later years: the ballet *Agon* (1953–4), and the musical play *The Flood*

(1961–2), based on the York and Chester mystery plays and first produced on American television.

Many of Stravinsky's later works, from the 1948 Mass onwards, sprang from religious impulses. They include *Threni* (*Lamentations of the Prophet Jeremiah*) for solo voices, chorus and orchestra (1957–8), the cantata *A Sermon, a Narrative and a Prayer* (1960–1), the "sacred ballad" *Abraham and Isaac* for baritone and chamber orchestra (1962–3), *Introitus* for men's voices and ensemble (1965), and his last major work, the *Requiem Canticles* for soloists, chorus and orchestra (1965–6). One of his last works was the charming setting for voice and piano of Edward Lear's poem "The Owl and the Pussy-Cat" (1966).

In 1969 Stravinsky and his wife moved to New York, where he died two years later. He was buried near Diaghilev in Venice.

ABOVE: The Rake's Progress *is a quasi-Mozartian full-length opera based on an English libretto. This photograph shows a 1952 performance at the Berlin State Opera.*

Sergei Prokofiev

I abhor imitation and I abhor the familiar.

PROKOFIEV

Prokofiev, together with Stravinsky and Shostakovich, belongs to the trio of great Russian composers of the 20th century. Like Stravinsky, he left Russia after the Revolution, settling in America and Paris, but unlike him, Prokofiev then returned in the 1930s, with mixed fortunes. He was a noted composer of stage music, but also – like Shostakovich – made significant contributions to both the symphonic and concerto repertoires.

Prokofiev was the only child of a wealthy and cultured family. He began to compose at five, and studied privately with Reinhold Glière (1875–1956). In September 1904 he entered the St Petersburg Conservatory, where he spent ten years. By the time of his public debut as a composer and pianist on New Year's Eve 1908, he was already an accomplished composer with a reputation for writing astringent, avant-garde music with a tendency to shock.

Prokofiev's life changed dramatically after his father's death in 1910, when he had to start earning a living. His response was to write the first of his five piano concertos, which caused uproar among critics. It was followed by a second (1913), which apparently left its listeners "frozen with fright, hair standing on end". Nevertheless, Prokofiev graduated from the Conservatory in June 1914 with the prestigious Rubinstein Prize.

ABOVE: Sergei Prokofiev, painted in 1934 by Pyotr Konchalovsky (1876–1956).

As a reward, his mother took him to London. There he met Diaghilev, who commissioned a ballet from him. Prokofiev's first attempt was a failure, and his second, *Chout* (*The Buffoon*), remained unperformed until 1921. Meanwhile Prokofiev had returned to a Russia torn by internal political strife and suffering from the deprivations of war. He spent the war years working on his opera *Igrok* (*The Gambler*, 1917, based on Dostoyevsky), the luminous First Violin Concerto (1916–17), and the ebullient, Haydnesque *Classical Symphony*, one of his most popular

works. When the political situation deteriorated after Lenin seized power, Prokofiev emigrated to the USA.

America and France

At first, his sensational piano-playing excited the American public, and the Chicago Opera commissioned the opera *The Love for Three Oranges* (which, after initial production problems, eventually became the only one of his ten or so operatic projects to achieve international success in his lifetime). But Prokofiev's performing career had stalled, and in 1922 he left for Paris, where he spent the next 14 years. His works of those years include three ballets, the Third, Fourth and Fifth Piano Concertos (the Fourth, written for Paul Wittgenstein in 1931, for left hand only), the Second Violin Concerto and the First Cello Concerto, and the Second, Third and Fourth Symphonies, as well as piano pieces and songs.

Return to Russia

By 1933 Prokofiev had received many invitations from his homeland, which he revisited several times. His decision to return permanently in 1936 was influenced by the increasing number of Russian commissions he was receiving, including the film music for *Lieutenant Kijé* (1934), and *Romeo and Juliet* for the Bolshoy Ballet (although

ABOVE, FROM LEFT TO RIGHT: *The conductor Ernst Ansermet, Diaghilev, Stravinsky and Prokofiev, c.1921.*

Prokofiev made a determined attempt to provide "Soviet realist" works which would satisfy Stalinist criteria. But these did not save him from oppression. During World War II his Spanish-born wife Lina was arrested on trumped-up charges of spying and sent to a labour camp under dubious circumstances; by then Prokofiev had formed a liaison with a Communist Party member, Mira Mendelson, with whom he lived until his death. In 1948 Prokofiev was among the composers denounced in the Stalinist press for "formalist perversions".

However, the best works of Prokofiev's "Soviet" period – the film score for Eisenstein's *Alexander Nevsky* (1938), the operas *Obrucheniye v Monastyre* (*The Duenna*, 1940–1, based on Sheridan), and *Voyna i mir* (*War and Peace*, 1941–3, based on Tolstoy), the Second String Quartet (1941), and the Fifth Symphony (1944) – remained true to his own artistic ideals. His last works included another Eisenstein film score, *Ivan the Terrible* (1945–7), the

ABOVE: *Prokofiev at work in the 1930s. He finally returned to Russia in 1936, having been enticed back by promising commissions.*

Sixth and Seventh Symphonies (1945–7), the ballets *Cinderella* (1940–4) and *Kamenniy tsvetok* (*The Tale of the Stone Flower*, 1948–53), and the Symphony-Concerto for cello and orchestra (1950–2), written for Mstislav Rostropovich (born 1927). Prokofiev died of a brain haemorrhage on the same day as Stalin.

the company initially rejected the score), but he chose an inopportune time to return, just as the Soviet authorities were beginning to interfere in artistic matters.

His first "Russian" works therefore included innocuous pieces, such as the much-loved *Peter and the Wolf* for children; and over the next decade

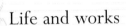

Life and works

NATIONALITY: Russian

BORN: Soutzovka, Ukraine, 1891; **DIED:** Moscow, 1953

SPECIALIST GENRES: Symphonies, concertos, stage works.

MAJOR WORKS: Seven symphonies, including *Classical Symphony* (1917); five piano concertos; two violin concertos; *The Love for Three Oranges* (1919); *Romeo and Juliet* (1935–6); *Peter and the Wolf* (1936); *War and Peace* (1941–3).

ABOVE: *The* pas de deux *from Prokofiev's ballet* Romeo and Juliet *(1935–6), written for the Bolshoy Ballet in Moscow. This performance took place at the Savonlinna Opera Festival in Finland.*

Paul Hindemith

Tell Hindemith that I am extremely pleased with him.

ARNOLD SCHOENBERG (1874–1951), 1924

The German-born composer, conductor, string player and teacher Paul Hindemith spent the early part of his career in Frankfurt, where he was a violinist in the Opera orchestra from 1915 until 1923, and where he studied composition at the Hoch Conservatory until 1917.

In 1921 two one-act operas, *Mörder, Hoffnung der Frauen* (*Murder, Hope of Women*), and *Das Nusch-Nuschi* (based on a play for Burmese marionettes), were performed in Stuttgart, where their scandalous subjects aroused controversy and gained notoriety for Hindemith. At the same time, the Amar Quartet (in which he played viola) was formed by the composer and Licco Amar to première his second String Quartet at the first Donaueschingen Festival, because the ensemble booked to play it had found it too difficult.

Two years later Hindemith was invited to join the festival's committee, and under his guidance it became Germany's leading festival for the promotion of new music. Meanwhile, Hindemith adopted an entirely different style: his series of seven works entitled *Kammermusik* ("chamber music") looked back to Baroque forms and polyphony. During the 1920s he taught at the Berlin Hochschule für Musik, and continued to play viola in the Amar Quartet. In 1929 he appeared at a London Promenade Concert as soloist in William Walton's Viola Concerto.

Although Hindemith was not Jewish, his wife was, and he was attacked by the Nazi party for the unacceptable

ABOVE: *The German composer Paul Hindemith (1895–1963).*

atonality of his music, and the fact that he openly associated with Jewish musicians. Despite the support of the conductor Wilhelm Furtwängler, who conducted the première of his *Mathis der Maler* Symphony in March 1934, Hindemith found himself on a list of proscribed composers. His opera *Mathis der Maler* (*Mathis the Painter*, based on the life of the 16th-century artist Grünewald), from which he had taken themes for the symphony, was banned by the Nazis and first performed in Switzerland in 1938.

As life in Nazi Germany became impossible, Hindemith joined the general exodus of talent. After some years teaching in Turkey, in 1939 he settled in New York, where he held

several university lectureships and was head of the school of music at Yale. In 1953 he settled in Switzerland. He died of pancreatitis in Frankfurt.

Hindemith was a prolific composer – almost too prolific for his own good. Concerned about the widening gap between the serious composer and the public, he was anxious that his music should be accessible to amateur players as well as professional performers. His works include a great deal of instrumental and educational music written with this in mind, and quantities of chamber music. His best-known works include the ballet *Nobilissima visione* (*Most Exalted Vision*) and the Rilke song-cycle *Das Marienleben* (*Scenes from the Life of Mary*). Many of his works are still neglected.

Life and works

NATIONALITY: German

BORN: Hanau, near Frankfurt, 1895; **DIED:** Frankfurt, 1963

SPECIALIST GENRES: Orchestral, chamber and piano music in German neo-classical idiom.

MAJOR WORKS: *Das Marienleben* (*Scenes from the Life of Mary*, 1922–3); operas *Cardillac* (1926) and *Mathis der Maler* (1933–4); *Nobilissima visione* (1938); *Symphonic Metamorphosis on Themes of Carl Maria von Weber* (1943).

William Walton

As a musical joker he is a jewel of the first water.

ERNEST NEWMAN (1868–1959), REVIEWING "FAÇADE"

The son of a Lancashire choirmaster and singing teacher, William Walton became a chorister at Christ Church, Oxford, when he was ten. At the age of 16 he entered Oxford University to read music, leaving two years later without a degree but having acquired a taste for high living. For the next decade he lived as the "adopted brother" of the eccentric Sitwell family in Chelsea and Italy, also spending lengthy periods at the homes of other wealthy admirers – which freed him to compose without the burden of having to earn a living. In 1920s London he associated with the "Fitzrovian" artistic community immortalized in Anthony Powell's series of novels *A Dance to the Music of Time*, which included the composers Lord Berners, Constant

Life and works

NATIONALITY: English

BORN: Oldham, 1902;
DIED: Ischia, 1983

SPECIALIST GENRES:
Orchestral music, film scores, stage music.

MAJOR WORKS:
Façade (1921–2); *Belshazzar's Feast* (1929–31); Symphony No. 1 (1935); Viola Concerto (1929); Violin Concerto (1938–9); *Troilus and Cressida* (1954).

ABOVE: William Walton, photographed towards the end of his life, in 1978. He was knighted in 1951.

Lambert and Peter Warlock. During these bohemian years Walton became keenly interested in jazz, and made his name with the satirical entertainment *Façade*, based on a number of witty poems by Edith Sitwell (1887–1964) and composed when he was only 19. It is still his most popular work.

Larger-scale works followed: the overture *Portsmouth Point* (1925), the Sinfonia Concertante (1926–7), and the Prokofiev-influenced Viola Concerto. In 1931 the oratorio *Belshazzar's Feast* burst upon the English choral scene at the Leeds Festival. Overnight Walton found himself acclaimed as Elgar's successor, a position he consolidated with his First Symphony, the Violin Concerto and the patriotic coronation march *Crown Imperial* (1937).

During the 1940s Walton concentrated on film music, a genre crowned by his three masterly Shakespearean collaborations with Laurence Olivier (*Henry V* in 1944, *Hamlet* in 1947, and *Richard III* in 1955). In 1948 he and his young Argentinian wife Susana Gil abandoned England for the idyllic Mediterranean island of Ischia. The early 1950s were chiefly occupied with his opera *Troilus and Cressida*, but its Covent Garden reception was disappointing. Later works included the Cello Concerto (1956), a Second Symphony (1959–60), and the *Missa brevis* (1966) written for Coventry Cathedral, but few recaptured the sparkle of Walton's earlier years. Knighted in 1951, he died aged 81, a pillar of the musical Establishment.

ABOVE: A poster for Laurence Olivier's film version of Shakespeare's Henry V *(1944), for which Walton provided a stirring score.*

Other Composers of the Era

Tonality is a natural force, like gravity.

PAUL HINDEMITH, "THE CRAFT OF MUSICAL COMPOSITION" (1937)

Spain produced its share of important 20th-century composers. Manuel de Falla (1876–1946) was much influenced by Spanish musical traditions, from Andalucian folk song to 16th-century Spanish polyphony. His one-act opera *La vida breve* (*Life is Short*) won a prize in Madrid in 1905, but was not produced until 1913 (in Nice), by which time Falla had been living in France for six years. In 1915 he wrote the ballet-pantomime *El amor brujo* (*Love the Magician*), but his fame was established in 1919 when Diaghilev produced the ballet *El sombrero de tres picos* (*The Three-cornered Hat*) in London. Falla's other major works include *Noches en los jardines de España* (*Nights in the Gardens of Spain*) for piano and orchestra (1916), the *Fantasia bética* for solo piano (1919), a Harpsichord

ABOVE: Ottorino Respighi (1879–1936), an Italian composer in the Romantic tradition.

Concerto (1926) and the chamber opera *El retablo de Maese Pedro* (*Master Peter's Puppet Show*, 1919–22). After the Spanish Civil War he moved to Argentina.

The Spanish composer Joaquín Rodrigo (1901–99), who taught music history at Madrid University from 1947 onwards, is chiefly known for two works for guitar and orchestra: the *Concierto de Aranjuez* (1939) and the *Fantasia para un gentilhombre* (1954). His other works, which include concertos for cello, piano, violin, flute, and multiple guitars, are less often performed.

Another popular, middle-of-the-road composer was the Italian Ottorino Respighi (1879–1936), who studied with Rimsky-Korsakov and ended up teaching at the Liceo di Santa Cecilia

in Rome, where he died. His richly scored tone-poems in the Straussian mould have always been popular, especially *Fontane di Roma* (*Fountains of Rome*, 1914–16), *Pini di Roma* (*Pines of Rome*, 1923–4), the *Trittico botticelliano* (*Three Botticelli Pictures*, 1927), *Gli uccelli* (*The Birds*, 1927), and *Feste romane* (*Roman Festivals*, 1928). His ballet *La boutique fantasque* (*The Marvellous Toyshop*, 1919) is based on Rossini transcriptions.

Britain

Walton's English contemporaries included a group of composers based in the Bloomsbury area of London – the "Fitzrovia" of Anthony Powell's novels. Powell's character Morland was based on the composer and conductor Constant Lambert (1905–51), who began his short but brilliant career

ABOVE: The Spanish composer Manuel de Falla (1876–1946) in 1924 in his studio in Granada, Andalucia.

ABOVE: The blind Spanish composer Joaquín Rodrigo (1901–99) playing the piano at his Madrid home, c.1975.

ABOVE: *The British composer and conductor Constant Lambert (1905–51) in the 1930s.*

with panache when his ballet *Romeo and Juliet* was commissioned by Diaghilev and performed in Monte Carlo in 1926. The next year, Lambert took London by storm with his irresistible, jazz-influenced cantata *The Rio Grande* for piano, chorus and orchestra, based on a poem by Sacheverell Sitwell (1897–1988). From 1941–7 he was music director of Sadler's Wells Ballet, and a one-time lover of the dancer Margot Fonteyn. His second wife

ABOVE: *Aram Khachaturian (1903–78), composer of* Spartacus *(used as theme music for the TV series "The Onedin Line").*

Isabel was a renowned artist and sculptress. Lambert's heavy drinking contributed to his early death. (His son Kit, who also died young, was the manager of the rock group The Who.)

One of Lambert's closest friends was the eccentric composer Philip Heseltine (1894–1930). Heseltine used his own name as an editor of early music, and the pseudonym "Peter Warlock" for performances and publication of his own compositions, which included many folk-song-influenced vocal settings, and the Renaissance-style *Capriol Suite* for string orchestra (1926). Warlock is presumed to have committed suicide.

Another eccentric English composer of the period was Gerald, Lord Berners (1883–1950), an aristocratic painter, author, diplomat and composer with a Satie-esque sense of humour. His best-known work is the ballet *The Triumph of Neptune* (1926), another Diaghilev commission.

Central Europe

The majority of German and Austrian Jewish composers managed to flee Nazism, but a notable group of Czech composers failed to survive the war. Among them was Ervín Schulhoff (1894–1942), who was interned at the Theresienstadt detention camp and then deported to Wülzbourg concentration camp, where he died. His works, which include eight symphonies, two string quartets, a sextet and four piano sonatas, show the influence of jazz and of other new developments.

While composers such as Prokofiev and Shostakovich managed to survive the Stalinist regime but still retain a strong individual voice, others bowed to the political pressure to produce music that the authorities would consider accessible to the masses. The Armenian composer Aram Khachaturian (1903–78) attracted Prokofiev's attention with his Trio for

ABOVE: *Peter Warlock, the pen-name of Philip Heseltine (1894–1930).*

piano, clarinet and violin, and achieved wide success with his First Symphony, his Piano Concerto and the 1942 ballet *Gayané* (which includes the popular "Sabre Dance"). His Second Violin Concerto, however, incurred official displeasure, and he abandoned serious composition in favour of neutral film scores. After Stalin's death he resumed his former career with the ballet *Spartacus*, premièred by the Kirov in 1956.

ABOVE: *The Czech composer Ervín Schulhoff (1894–1942), one of the most prominent musical victims of the Nazis.*

Music
✤ since ✤
World War II

A recording studio in Hollywood. Electronic studios were first used by post-war composers such as Edgard Varèse, Luciano Berio and Karlheinz Stockhausen.

Modern Music

The serial idea is based on a universe that finds itself in perpetual expansion.

PIERRE BOULEZ (BORN 1925)

From the late 20th century, music has become more fragmentary than at any previous historical period. There are no longer "schools" of composition: each composer now strives to find an original and entirely individual voice. If they draw inspiration from other music, it is from the works of individual predecessors rather than from general trends.

Both Shostakovich and Benjamin Britten came into their own after 1945, the year that Britten revitalized British opera with *Peter Grimes*. While Britten's principal importance lies in vocal music, especially his fine sequence of operas, Shostakovich was primarily an instrumental composer. Both were inspired by the playing of the Russian cellist Mstislav Rostropovich, for whom Shostakovich wrote his cello concertos and Britten his Cello Symphony and three solo suites. Both composers worked in an essentially tonal medium, unaffected by avant-garde developments.

Britain has maintained a strong operatic tradition since 1945, in the works of Britten, Michael Tippett, Harrison Birtwistle, Peter Maxwell Davies, and now a younger generation of composers, including Mark-Anthony Turnage and Thomas Adès. In America, Leonard Bernstein revitalized the American musical, especially with his brilliant *West Side Story* (1957), but has proved perhaps more influential as a conductor than as a composer. Meanwhile, Copland (though active up until his death) ceded the mantle of senior American composer to Elliott

ABOVE: VE Day, 8 May 1945. Crowds in Whitehall, London, cheering Prime Minister Winston Churchill and members of the Cabinet after the announcement of Germany's surrender.

ABOVE: The first landing on the Moon — the Apollo 11 mission, 1969.

Carter, whose orchestral and chamber music is characterized by the most rigorous intellectual discipline and formal perfection.

Minimalism

The experiments of John Cage proved a blind alley in themselves (the notorious *4' 33"* took music to its furthest extreme – complete silence), but Cage's ideas have taken root, most obviously in the American minimalist school of Steve Reich, Terry Riley, Philip Glass and John Adams, whose music relies on repetitive rhythmic and melodic *ostinati* for its hypnotic effect. The fact that such music has connections with the harmonic and rhythmic clichés of pop and rock music, as well as with Indian and African music (popular in the West since the 1960s), has contributed to its popularity. The British composer Michael Nyman (born 1944) uses similar techniques in his film scores.

Electronic music

Cage's use of aleatory, or chance, techniques (derived from the Chinese *I-Ching*, or *The Book of Changes*) has been independently adopted and developed to a limited extent by the Polish composer Witold Lutoslawski, and in a more intensely focused way by the Greek composer Iannis Xenakis, many of whose works use electronic tape. The use of electronic instruments, amplification and sampling has become widespread in "serious" music over the last 50 years. Composers who have

ABOVE: *The American composer Philip Glass (born 1937) rehearsing with musicians in Los Angeles, March 1977.*

ABOVE: *Students using computers on the Electro-Acoustic Composition Course at Dartington, 1999.*

made use of such techniques include the early Franco-American experimenter Edgard Varèse, the Italians Luciano Berio and Bruno Maderna, the British composer Jonathan Harvey, and the German Karlheinz Stockhausen, one of the leaders of the European avant-garde in the 1960s and '70s.

French music in the later 20th century was dominated by two composers. The idiosyncratic style of Olivier Messiaen was influenced by Eastern music, birdsong, the serial technique of Webern – which he refined still further – and his profound Catholic faith. His pupil Pierre Boulez, who founded the major European research centre into modern composing techniques, is a central figure in 20th–21st-century European music. Equally well-known as a conductor, he has helped to co-ordinate the work of composers from many different countries, as well as producing an important and highly original body of work rooted in the French tradition, but cross-fertilized by European avant-garde techniques.

Female composers

One encouraging feature of music in recent years has been the emergence of women composers, and the rediscovery, after centuries of neglect, of the music of talented women of the past, such as Fanny Mendelssohn (1805–47) and Amy Beach (1867–1944). Composers such as Judith Weir (born 1954), Sofia Gubaidulina (born 1931), Elena Firsova (born 1950) and Roxanna Panufnik (born 1968) are now beginning to challenge the traditional male hegemony in composition, as in many other fields, and are proving particularly adept in the developing fields of television and film music.

ABOVE: *Kurt Masur conducting the New York Philharmonic in the Avery Fisher Hall, New York, 1998.*

Dmitri Shostakovich

*The music [Symphony No. 11] to me was self-evidently about
Shostakovich's own experiences in the catastrophe of his life.*

MICHAEL TIPPETT (1905–98)

Together with Stravinsky and Prokofiev, Shostakovich was one of the greatest Russian composers of the 20th century. His 15 symphonies and 15 string quartets are among the finest 20th-century works in those media.

Shostakovich began to learn the piano with his mother, a professional pianist. In 1919, aged only 13, he entered the St Petersburg Conservatory to study piano and composition: his teachers there included Glazunov. A phenomenally gifted student, his First Symphony (written as a diploma exercise) won international acclaim after its premières in Leningrad (1926), Berlin (under Bruno Walter), and Philadelphia (under Leopold Stokowski); a year later Shostakovich received an honourable mention as an entrant in the International Chopin Piano Competition.

During the 1920s Shostakovich – a firm adherent to Socialist ideals – concentrated on stage and film music. An opera, *Nos* (*The Nose*), and two

ABOVE: *Dmitri Shostakovich (1906–75), photographed at the Moscow Conservatory in the early 1960s.*

ballets, *Zolotoy vek* (*The Golden Age*, 1927–30) and *Bolt* (1930–1), showed him developing a brittle, witty and satirical style which owed much to current European avant-garde

influences, and for several years he was regarded as the "great white hope" of Soviet music.

Denunciation

Then came catastrophe. His opera *Lady Macbeth of the Mtsensk District*, a savage tale of adultery, murder and retribution, was produced in Moscow in 1934. At first it won critical acceptance both within Russia and abroad. But Stalin went to see it and was shocked by its graphic portrayal of sex and violence, and by its "advanced" musical idiom. On his orders, Shostakovich was savagely attacked in the press in 1936, in an article entitled "Chaos instead of Music".

Denounced also by his fellow composers, Shostakovich hurriedly withdrew the score of his Fourth Symphony, then in rehearsal, and responded with the more "accessible" Fifth Symphony (1937), which he described as "A Soviet artist's response to just criticism". For a while he

LEFT:
*Shostakovich
composing at
his Moscow flat.*

RIGHT:
*A view of the
Admiralty in St
Petersburg, where
Shostakovich
was born and
where he
studied.*

appeared to have been forgiven: the Fifth Symphony proved popular, his 1940 Piano Quintet received the Stalin Prize, and his Seventh Symphony, written during the German siege of Leningrad in 1941, became an international symbol of heroic resistance (even though its repetitive "invasion" theme was cruelly parodied by Bartók in his Concerto for Orchestra, written in America in 1943).

Shostakovich's next two symphonies were also inspired by the war: the Eighth (1943) by its savagery, and the Ninth (1945) in a spirit of rejoicing at its end. But in 1948 he was once again officially denounced (together with Prokofiev and others), accused of "formalist perversions" and "anti-democratic tendencies in music". Such denunciations, during the Stalinist purges of the late 1940s, were tantamount to a death sentence, and if Shostakovich's posthumously published *Memoirs* are to be believed, from then until Stalin's death in 1953 he lived in fear for his life. He kept his private artistic credo alive with intimate chamber works, while publicly he concentrated on "safe" works based on nationalistic themes.

ABOVE, FROM LEFT TO RIGHT: *The great Russian cellist Mstislav Rostropovich (for whom Shostakovich wrote his cello concertos), Shostakovich, Rostropovich's wife — the soprano Galina Vishnevskaya — and the violinist David Oistrakh.*

The post-Stalin era

After Stalin's death, Shostakovich returned to symphonic writing with the Tenth, Eleventh (*The Year 1905*) and Twelfth (*The Year 1917*) Symphonies. The late 1950s also produced the satirical musical comedy *Cheryomuschki* (*The Cherry Trees Estate*, 1958), a suite, *The Gadfly*, from his film score of 1955, the Second Piano Concerto (written in 1957 for his son Maxim, who became a well-known conductor), the First Cello Concerto (written in 1959 for Rostropovich), and the Seventh and Eighth String Quartets (1960).

In 1962 *Lady Macbeth* was restored to the Russian repertoire (under the new title *Katerina Ismailova*) and hailed as a masterpiece. Shostakovich then produced another controversial work, the Thirteenth Symphony (*Babi Yar*), based on poems by the Jewish writer Yevgeny Yevtushenko (born 1933). Its two successors, particularly the anguished Fourteenth Symphony of 1969 (settings of 11 poems by European writers), are preoccupied with death: the Fifteenth Symphony (1971), with its ironic references to other composers, seems to sum up

Shostakovich's own career. The last decade of his life produced seven more string quartets, sonatas for violin and viola, and a further concerto each for violin and cello.

Towards the end of his life, Shostakovich was allowed to visit the West. He became a friend of Benjamin Britten, to whom the Fourteenth Symphony is dedicated. Like Britten, he died of heart failure in his 60s.

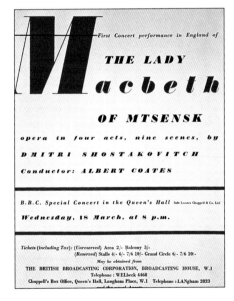

ABOVE: *A programme for the first London concert performance of Shostakovich's opera* Lady Macbeth of Mtsensk, *in 1935.*

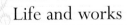

Life and works

NATIONALITY: Russian

BORN: St Petersburg, 1906;
DIED: Moscow, 1975

SPECIALIST GENRES:
Symphonies, concertos, string quartets, operas.

MAJOR WORKS: 15 symphonies; concertos for piano, violin and cello; chamber music, including 15 string quartets; operas *The Nose* (1927–8) and *Lady Macbeth of the Mtsensk District* (1934).

Benjamin Britten

If wind and water could write music, it would sound like Ben's.

YEHUDI MENUHIN (1916–99)

Together with Michael Tippett, Britten dominated the British musical scene from the 1930s onwards. His roots lay in the music of Mozart and Verdi, and he never abandoned tonality, but he developed a distinctive style with wide appeal. Much of his music was inspired by specific performers, particularly the tenor voice of his lifelong companion, Peter Pears (1910–86).

Britten was born on St Cecilia's Day, 22 November 1913. He went to boarding school, but studied composition privately with Frank Bridge (1879–1941) in school holidays. In 1930 he entered the Royal College of Music in London, where he studied composition with John Ireland and honed his already formidable skills as a pianist. He wanted to continue his studies in Vienna with Alban Berg,

ABOVE: Benjamin Britten, one of the major British composers of the 20th century.

having heard Berg's opera *Wozzeck* in 1934, but was discouraged by his parents and teachers.

Early works
In 1935, by which time several early works including a Sinfonietta and an Oboe Quartet had already been performed, Britten began to work for the documentary film unit of the General Post Office, where he met the poet W. H. Auden. They shared left-wing political sympathies and collaborated on several works, including the orchestral song-cycle *Our Hunting Fathers* (1936) and the choral work *Ballad of Heroes* (1939). In that year Britten and Peter Pears followed Auden to the USA. By this time Britten's natural predilection for vocal music had already been confirmed with the Rimbaud song-cycle *Les illuminations* (1939), but the

Seven Sonnets of Michelangelo of 1940 was the first of many works which Britten wrote expressly for Pears. Instrumental works of the late 1930s and early '40s included the charming Rossini pastiche *Soirées musicales* (1936), the brilliant *Variations on a Theme of Frank Bridge* for strings (1937), concertos for piano (1938) and violin (1940), and the *Sinfonia da requiem* (1940). From then onwards, Britten wrote few specifically orchestral works. Exceptions were the *Young Person's Guide to the Orchestra* (1946) and the exquisite Serenade for tenor, horn and strings (1943, written

ABOVE: Britten (left) with his lifelong companion Peter Pears in the garden of their house at Aldeburgh, Suffolk. This was one of the last photographs of Britten.

Life and works

NATIONALITY: English

BORN: Lowestoft, 1913;
DIED: Aldeburgh, 1976

SPECIALIST GENRES: Opera and other stage works, vocal music.

MAJOR WORKS: Operas *Peter Grimes* (1944–5), *Billy Budd* (1951), *The Turn of the Screw* (1954), *A Midsummer Night's Dream* (1960) and *Death in Venice* (1973); *War Requiem* (1962); three "church parables"; chamber music and songs, including song-cycles and folk song arrangements.

for Pears and the horn player Dennis Brain), two of his most popular works; the Cello Symphony for Rostropovich (1963); and two "occasional" works written to celebrate the respective openings of the Snape Maltings concert hall and the Queen Elizabeth Hall in London.

Aldeburgh Festival

Britten decided to return home from America in 1942, having by chance read George Crabbe's 19th-century poem *The Borough*, an unflattering portrait of the Suffolk fishing village of Aldeburgh, which inspired his first major opera, *Peter Grimes*. Its première at Sadler's Wells on 7 June 1945 marked a milestone in British music, and in the history of opera. Britten and Pears settled first at Snape, a few miles inland, and then in Aldeburgh itself, where in 1947 they established the annual Aldeburgh Festival. Twenty years later, the festival's main venue moved from Aldeburgh's tiny Jubilee Hall to a converted malthouse at Snape.

Opera and choral works

Three original chamber operas followed *Peter Grimes*: *The Rape of Lucretia* (1946), the comedy *Albert Herring* (1947), both performed at Glyndebourne, and *The Little Sweep* (1949). In 1951, *Billy Budd* (based on Herman Melville's nautical tragedy) was performed at Covent Garden, followed two years later by Britten's one failure, *Gloriana* (intended to celebrate Elizabeth II's accession in 1953): later productions have led to its reassessment. *The Turn of the Screw*, based on Henry James's ghost story, was premièred in Venice, the city which inspired Britten's operatic swansong (and the most direct expression of his love for Pears), *Death in Venice*, based on Thomas Mann's novella. Many people

ABOVE: The Maltings at Snape, converted by Britten's efforts from an abandoned malthouse to a fine concert hall, the major venue for the Aldeburgh Festival.

consider his operatic masterpiece to be the Shakespearean *A Midsummer Night's Dream*.

During the 1960s Britten temporarily eschewed conventional operas in favour of three "church parables" written for performance in Orford Church in Suffolk: *Curlew River* (1964, inspired by Japanese Noh drama), *The Burning Fiery Furnace* (1966) and *The Prodigal Son* (1968). His next opera, *Owen Wingrave*, was written for television in 1970, though it subsequently transferred successfully to the stage. In 1962

his *War Requiem* was performed at the newly opened Coventry Cathedral, with an international cast of soloists, in a spirit of post-war reconciliation. The Requiem text is interwoven with the poetry of Wilfred Owen (1893–1918), and the work is a powerful expression of Britten's pacifism.

Besides composing, Britten was a fine conductor and pianist, and often toured in recital with Pears. In 1973 he had heart surgery, which curtailed his activities, and shortly before his death in 1976 he became the first British composer to be made a life peer.

ABOVE: A scene from the 1995 Covent Garden production of Peter Grimes, *with Bryn Terfel as Captain Balstrode, and Ben Heppner as the fisherman Grimes.*

Michael Tippett

I like to think of composing as a physical business. I compose at the piano
and like to feel involved in my work with my hands.

TIPPETT

Like his younger contemporary Benjamin Britten, the English composer Michael Tippett grew up in Suffolk, and studied at the Royal College of Music in London. He left in 1928 and became a schoolteacher and part-time composer. His first mature works were the First String Quartet (1935), the First Piano Sonata (1936–7), and the Concerto for Double String Orchestra (1938–9), which belongs to the early 20th-century British tradition of works for string ensemble.

During the 1930s Tippett became involved in radical politics, organizing the "South London Orchestra of Unemployed Musicians". His passionate antipathy towards the horrors of war, initially aroused by the plight of European Jews, found expression in his deeply moving oratorio based on the true story of a Jewish boy who killed

ABOVE: For the last two decades of Michael Tippett's life he was the undisputed "Grand Old Man" of British music.

a Nazi diplomat, *A Child of Our Time* (1939–41), which articulates Tippett's lifelong belief in the opposing "dark" and "light" sides of human nature, present in everyone. The oratorio is influenced by Bach's Passions, with negro spirituals replacing Protestant chorales. Tippett was briefly imprisoned for his pacifist beliefs in 1943.

From 1940–51 Tippett was director of music at Morley College in South London. He subsequently became a full-time composer. His first opera, *The Midsummer Marriage*, was produced in 1952, and like each of its successors – *King Priam* (1961), *The Knot Garden* (1970), *The Ice Break* (1976), *New Year* (1989) – it spawned instrumental and

vocal works, including an important series of five string quartets, four symphonies, four piano sonatas and the *Songs for Dov* (1969–70) for tenor and chamber orchestra.

In 1995, the year of his 90th birthday, a Tippett Festival at the Barbican in London included the première of his last major work, *The Rose Lake*, a "song without words for orchestra". His last work was "Caliban's Song", part of a *Tempest Suite* commissioned by the BBC to mark the tercentenary of Purcell's death. Renaissance and Baroque music had been a major influence on Tippett's earlier works, including the *Fantasia Concertante on a Theme of Corelli* for strings (1953).

ABOVE: Tippett composing at the piano in 1992. His sight failed in the last years of his life.

Life and works

NATIONALITY: English

BORN: London, 1905;
DIED: London, 1998

SPECIALIST GENRES: Opera, symphonies, string quartets.

MAJOR WORKS: Concerto for Double String Orchestra (1938–9); *A Child of Our Time* (1939–41); five operas, including *The Midsummer Marriage* (1952); Piano Concerto (1953–5); *The Vision of St Augustine* (1965); *The Mask of Time* (1980–2); four symphonies; five string quartets.

John Cage

It is better to make a piece of music than to perform one.

CAGE, "SILENCE" (1961)

The American composer John Cage was one of the most interesting experimental artists of his time. He studied with Henry Cowell (1897–1965, himself a noted pioneer of innovative techniques) and with Schoenberg, who called him "an inventor – of genius". From 1937 onwards he developed a strong interest in dance and percussion techniques, and in 1942 he moved from the West Coast to New York, where he began a long association with Merce Cunningham's dance company.

In 1938 he invented the "prepared piano" by inserting small domestic objects such as paperclips and rubber bands between the strings. This instrument, capable of producing extraordinary timbres, was used in Cage's early pieces such as *Sonatas and*

ABOVE: *Experimental composer John Cage, more a "musical philosopher" than a composer.*

Interludes (1946–8), and *Music for Marcel Duchamp* (1947). *The Wonderful Widow of Eighteen Springs* (1942) is a setting of a poem by James Joyce for voice and closed piano. A devotee of Zen Buddhism (before it became fashionable) and the *I-Ching*, Cage introduced aleatory (chance) techniques into his music, for instance in *Music of Changes* for piano (1951), in which the performance depends on the toss of a coin, and *Cheap Imitation* (1969), an alteration of Satie's *Socrate*, worked out using the *I-Ching*. With these works, he changed the nature of music by removing the necessity of intention from composition.

In 1952, with *Imaginary Landscape V*, Cage began to use electronic tape in his works. In the same year he "wrote" his notorious *4' 33"*, in which the performer sits at a silent piano and is required only to indicate the division

of the work into three movements: the attention of the audience is directed to life (including the chance sounds of the environment) rather than art. Also from 1952 dates *Theater Piece* for Merce Cunningham, the first "musical happening", combining theatre, art and music. From then on Cage used a wide range of electronic media in his works, which are often scored for bizarre combinations. For example, *Imaginary Landscape IV* (1951) is for 12 radios and 24 players, *Speech* (1955) for five radios and newsreader, *HPSCHD* (1967–9) for seven harpsichord soloists and 51 tape machines, and *Postcard from Heaven* (1983) for between one and 20 harpsichords.

Cage was a musical philosopher. He believed that art was whatever the artist said it was: "I have nothing to say, I am saying it, and that is poetry." An avowed anarchist, he followed a strict macrobiotic diet, was a brilliant chess player and an expert on mushrooms.

ABOVE: *One of the "instruments" used in the performance by Ensemble Bash of* The Art of Concealment *for percussion ensemble.*

Life and works

NATIONALITY: American

BORN: Los Angeles, 1912; **DIED:** New York, 1992

SPECIALIST GENRES: Experimental works for bizarre combinations.

MAJOR WORKS: Numerous works for percussion ensemble, prepared piano and various combinations of instruments and electronic media.

Leonard Bernstein

Any composer's writing is the sum of himself, of all his roots and influences.

BERNSTEIN, "THE JOY OF MUSIC" (1960)

Bernstein was one of the most flamboyant figures of 20th-century music. A talented pianist, composer of both "serious" works and extremely popular Broadway musicals and one of the finest conductors of his age, he excelled in every field he tackled (one of his fellow students remarked that he was "doomed to success").

He studied composition at Harvard University with Walter Piston (1894–1976), and conducting with Fritz Reiner (1888–1963) at the Curtis Institute in Philadelphia; in the early 1940s he attended summer schools at Tanglewood, Massachusetts, where he became Serge Koussevitzky's assistant. He was then invited to become assistant conductor of the New York Philharmonic Orchestra, and his big break came in November 1943, when he took over a concert at short notice from the indisposed Bruno Walter. This triumphant performance launched his career, helped by his striking good looks and charismatic personality.

From 1946 onwards Bernstein began to conduct opera, beginning with the US première of Britten's *Peter Grimes* at Tanglewood. In 1953 he became the first American to conduct at La Scala in Milan. He made his debut at the Metropolitan Opera House in 1964, and from 1958–69 he was principal conductor of the New York Philharmonic. He also guest-conducted many of the world's great orchestras.

Bernstein's parallel career as a composer began in 1944 with his ballet *Fancy Free* and his musical *On the Town*, which ran for 463 performances on Broadway. An adaptation of Voltaire's *Candide* (1954–6) had a disappointing reception and was later revised, but *West Side Story* (1957) made Bernstein's name. Written in collaboration with Stephen Sondheim (born 1930) and the choreographer Jerome Robbins (born 1918), this brilliant adaptation of the *Romeo and Juliet* story to a modern New York slum setting captured the spirit of the age.

The bisexual Bernstein was married to the Chilean actress Felicia Montealegre Cohn in 1951, and had three children.

ABOVE: Leonard Bernstein, photographed in the late 1960s.

LEFT: The ensemble song "America" from West Side Story, *as performed at the Prince Edward Theatre in London in 1998.*

Life and works

NATIONALITY: American

BORN: Lawrence, Massachusetts, 1918;
DIED: New York, 1990

SPECIALIST GENRES: Populist stage works (ballets and musicals).

MAJOR WORKS: *On the Town* (1944); *Prelude, Fugue and Riffs* for clarinet and jazz ensemble (1949); *Candide* (1956); *West Side Story* (1957); *Chichester Psalms* (1965); *1600 Pennsylvania Avenue* (1976); three symphonies.

Elliott Carter

I am a radical, having a nature that leads me to perpetual revolt.

CARTER, C.1939

After Copland's death in 1990, Elliott Carter assumed the mantle of "Grand Old Man of American Music". But although he too studied with Nadia Boulanger in Paris in the early 1930s, his musical approach (apart from early works such as the First Symphony and the *Holiday Overture*) is very different from Copland's.

On returning to the USA after his Paris studies Carter became a musical director of Ballet Caravan (1936–40), and then began a long and distinguished teaching career in many major American universities and institutions. He has also spent long periods abroad, including fellowships of the American Academy in Rome, where he composed his Variations for Orchestra (1954–5). The Concerto for

Orchestra and the Third String Quartet (1971) were also written in Italy.

Carter's output includes choral music, songs (including "Warble for Lilac Time", 1943, "A Mirror on Which to Dwell", 1975, and "In Sleep, In Thunder", 1981) and incidental music (including the 1937–9 ballet *Pocahontas*). But his most significant works are for orchestra or chamber groups, particularly the five string quartets, which are regarded

as the most important since Bartók's. He is fascinated by the rhythmic and harmonic possibilities inherent in combining ensembles, as in the Symphony of Three Orchestras, the *Penthode* for five instrumental quartets (1984–5), and the Triple Duo (1982–3). The impact of experimental, radical influences on his underlying classical training has resulted in music of apparent complexity, underpinned by an inexorable musical logic of profound simplicity. The fusion of slow-moving formal structures with ebullient momentum gives Carter's work great dramatic power. His later works include an Oboe Concerto (1986–7) and Violin Concerto (1990), *Three Occasions* for orchestra (the third celebrated his own 50th wedding anniversary in 1989); and works for solo instruments, including *Changes* for guitar (1983), *Trilogy* (1992) for oboe and harp, and *Gra* (1993) for clarinet. A quintet for piano and wind, one of his finest later works, dates from 1992.

Life and works

NATIONALITY: American

BORN: New York, 1908

SPECIALIST GENRES: Complex polyrhythmic works.

MAJOR WORKS: Ballets *Pocahontas* (1937–9) and *The Minotaur* (1947); Piano Sonata (1946); Double Concerto for harpsichord and piano (1961); Concerto for Orchestra (1969); Symphony of Three Orchestras (1976–7); five string quartets.

ABOVE:
The American composer Elliott Carter (born 1908).

RIGHT: Carter rehearsing his Triple Duo at the Royal Academy of Music in London.

Witold Lutoslawski

Dissonances are only the more remote consonances.

ARNOLD SCHOENBERG (1874–1951)

Lutoslawski was the major Polish composer of the 20th century. He began to compose at the age of nine, and also studied piano and violin. In 1932 he entered the Warsaw Conservatory, and two years later his Piano Sonata was broadcast on Polish Radio. His Symphonic Variations were performed at the 1939 Krakow Festival.

The war disrupted Lutoslawski's promising career. He was taken prisoner, but escaped and eked out a precarious living playing the piano in Warsaw cafés. Many of his manuscripts disappeared during the wartime devastation: one exception was the *Variations on a Theme of Paganini* for two pianos, which Lutoslawski adapted in 1978 for piano and orchestra. In post-war communist Poland he wrote music for radio, film and television, and folk-based music for children. His First Symphony (1949) was denounced as formalist, and banned for a decade, but his Little Suite for orchestra (1950) and the Concerto for Orchestra (1950–4) – a worthy successor to Bartók's – found acceptance.

In the post-Stalinist thaw, Lutoslawski began to enlarge his harmonic language, exploring different ways of using the notes of the scale. *Funeral Music* (1958), dedicated to Bartók, established his international reputation, and his works of the 1960s, such as *Jeux vénitiens* (*Venetian Games*, 1961), *Trois poèmes d'Henri Michaux* (1963) and the 1964 String Quartet began to experiment with chance elements. His most

important works of the late 1970s include *Paroles tissées* (*Woven Words*, 1965, written for Peter Pears), the Second Symphony (1967), *Livre pour orchestre* (1968), the Cello Concerto (1970, for Rostropovich), Preludes and Fugue for 13 solo strings, *Les espaces du sommeil* (*Sleep's Spaces*, 1975) for baritone and orchestra, and *Mi-parti* (1976).

Many works were commissioned by major artists and ensembles, including the Third Symphony by the Chicago Symphony Orchestra, *Chain I* by the London Sinfonietta, *Chain II* by the violinist Anne-Sophie Mutter (born 1963), and *Chain III* for the San Francisco Symphony Orchestra.

Lutoslawski's last major works included a Piano Concerto (1988), *Interludium* for chamber orchestra (1989) and *Chantefables et chantefleurs* (1990) for soprano and orchestra.

ABOVE: Witold Lutoslawski, the most important Polish composer of his generation.

LEFT: Lutoslawski rehearsing at the Royal Academy of Music in London in 1980.

Life and works

NATIONALITY: Polish

BORN: Warsaw, 1913;
DIED: Warsaw, 1994

SPECIALIST GENRES: Orchestral works.

MAJOR WORKS: Concerto for Orchestra (1954); *Funeral Music* (1958); Cello Concerto (1970); four symphonies; Piano Concerto (1988).

György Ligeti

*It is precisely a dread of deep significance and ideology that makes
any kind of engaged art out of the question for me.*

LIGETI

One of Hungary's most important composers, Ligeti was born in Transylvania of Hungarian Jewish parents, and studied privately during the war in Budapest. After the war he went to the Budapest Academy of Music, where from 1950–6 he was a professor. He left Hungary in 1956, the year of the Soviet invasion, and took up residence in Vienna. He was invited to work at the West German Radio electronic studios in Cologne, and caused a sensation at the 1960 International Society for Contemporary Music Festival with *Apparitions* (1958–9). From 1959 onwards he taught annually on the summer courses for new music at Darmstadt. Ten years later he moved to West Berlin, and from 1973–89 he was professor of composition at the Hamburg Musikhochschule.

ABOVE: The Hungarian composer György Ligeti (born 1923), photographed in 1993.

Ligeti's early works were influenced by folk song and the music of Bartók. After a few experiments with electronic media in the late 1950s, he began to find an individual style in works such as *Apparitions* and *Atmosphères* for orchestra (1961), *Volumina* for organ (1961–2), and with the two works for solo voices and instruments called *Aventures* and *Nouvelles aventures* (1962–5). His works of the 1960s included a Requiem (1963–5), a Cello Concerto (1966), *Lux aeterna* for 16 solo voices (1966), the orchestral work *Lontano* (1967) and a chamber concerto for 13 instruments (1969–70). Some of his music was used – without

his permission – in the score of Stanley Kubrick's 1968 film *2001: A Space Odyssey*. Since the 1960s, Ligeti's most significant works have been *Clocks and Clouds* for 12-voice women's chorus and orchestra, *Melodien* (1971) and *San Francisco Polyphony* (1973–4), both for orchestra, a Double Concerto for flute and oboe (1972), a Piano Concerto (1985–8), a Violin Concerto (1992), a Horn Trio, subtitled "Homage to Brahms" (1982), a set of piano Etudes (1985), and the opera *Le grand macabre*. His individual style, which the composer describes as "micropolyphony", is derived from Webern.

ABOVE: "The Horse of the Apocalypse" being prepared in rehearsal for a performance of Ligeti's opera Le grand macabre *at the 1997 Salzburg Festival.*

Life and works

NATIONALITY: Hungarian

BORN: Kolozsvár (now Cluj in Romania), 1923

SPECIALIST GENRES: Orchestral and chamber music.

MAJOR WORKS: *Atmosphères* (1961); *Aventures* (1962); *Le grand macabre* (1972–6); *Clocks and Clouds* (1972).

Olivier Messiaen

Fantastic music of the stars.

KARLHEINZ STOCKHAUSEN (BORN 1928)

ABOVE: The French composer Olivier Messiaen, photographed in 1937.

One of the most idiosyncratic composers of the 20th century, Messiaen was the son of an English teacher and a poet. He began to compose at the age of seven and, after discovering the music of Debussy, he decided at an early age to become a composer. He studied at the Paris Conservatoire from the age of 11, winning four first prizes in piano, history of music and composition, and during his last years there he wrote his Preludes for piano in the style of Debussy.

After graduating, Messiaen became organist at La Trinité in Paris, where he stayed for over 40 years. He also taught at the Ecole Normale de Musique, the Schola Cantorum, and the Paris Conservatoire (where he became professor of composition in 1966). He was a profoundly influential teacher: his pupils included Boulez, Stockhausen, Xenakis and Alexander Goehr (born 1932, who later taught at Cambridge University).

Religious inspiration

Many of Messiaen's compositions celebrate love, both human and divine. The influence of his Catholic faith is omnipresent in his works, many of which take the form of religious "meditations", "homages" or acts of praise. Far from shying away from explicitly religious titles, as other composers in this predominantly secular age have done, Messiaen made his intention clear, in orchestral pieces such as *Les offrandes oubliées* (*Forgotten offerings*, 1930), *Hymne au Saint Sacrement* (1932), *Et exspecto resurrectionem mortuorum* (*And I Await the Resurrection of the Dead*, 1964) and *Eclairs sur l'au-delà* (*Illuminations of the Beyond*, 1988–92). His early *Quatuor pour la fin du temps* (*Quartet for the End of Time*) for clarinet, violin, cello and piano was written and first performed in a Silesian prison camp where Messiaen was interned by the Germans for two years during World War II. Vocal works on religious themes include the early Mass (1933), *Trois petites liturgies de la présence divine* (1944) and *La transfiguration de Notre Seigneur Jésus-Christ* (1965–9).

Messiaen's keyboard works have also been inspired by his faith, including *Vingt regards sur l'enfant Jésus-Christ* (1944) for piano; and a series of fine organ works including *L'ascension* (1934), *La nativité du Seigneur* (1935), *Méditation sur le mystère de la Sainte Trinité* (1969) and the *Livre du Saint Sacrement* (1984). His only opera, completed in 1983, was based on the life of St Francis of Assisi.

Other influences

While profoundly religious, Messiaen was equally alive to the force of human passion. *Poèmes pour Mi* (1936), for soprano and piano or orchestra, was written in celebration of his marriage to the violinist Claire Delbos. *Harawi* —

ABOVE: Messiaen with the score of his Turangalîla-Symphonie *at the Oxford Festival in June 1967.*

ABOVE: Messiaen rehearsing with students at the Royal Academy of Music in London, 1987.

songs of love and death with elements taken from Peruvian folk music – for soprano and piano, *Cinq rechants* (*Five Refrains*) for 12 solo voices, and the massive orchestral *Turangalîla-Symphonie* form a trilogy of works with a powerful erotic charge.

Another major influence was that of birdsong. Messiaen was an expert ornithologist and made a systematic, classified study of all French birds, recording and notating their songs. Their characteristic rhythmic and melodic patterns were transmuted into his own music in specific works such as *Réveil des oiseaux* (*Dawn Chorus*, 1953) and *Oiseaux exotiques* (1955–6) for orchestra, *Catalogue d'oiseaux* (1956–8) and *Petites esquisses d'oiseaux* (*Little Bird Sketches*, 1985) for piano, and *Le merle noir* (*The Blackbird*, 1951) for flute and piano. Elements of birdsong are found in most of his works.

Messiaen's music

Messiaen's musical language is immensely complex. He set out its principles in his book, *Technique de mon langage musical* (1944), which analyses the derivations of its rhythmic structures from Hindu and ancient Greek rhythms. His orchestral works are characterized by luscious harmonies and a vast range of timbres, some derived from exotic percussion instruments including the *ondes Martenot*, an electronic instrument played by Messiaen's second wife, the virtuoso pianist Yvonne Loriod. His fascination with colour and timbre is explored in many works, including *Chronochromie* (*Time-colour*) for orchestra (1960), *Couleurs de la cité céleste* (*Colours of the Celestial City*, 1963), and many of his organ works. His last orchestral work (1989) was entitled *Un sourire* (*A Smile*).

ABOVE: Much of Messiaen's music was influenced by birdsong.

Pierre Boulez

Music should be a collective magic and hysteria.

BOULEZ

ABOVE: *Pierre Boulez (born 1925), photographed in 1999.*

Messiaen's most talented pupil was Pierre Boulez, who studied with him at the Paris Conservatoire after moving to Paris in 1942 from his native Montbrison in the Loire region. Boulez was originally destined for a career in engineering, but instead applied his exceptional mathematical brain to musical analysis and composition.

Twelve-note technique, which Boulez studied in the late 1940s with Schoenberg's pupil René Leibowitz (1913–72), influenced his own early works, the Sonatina for flute and piano (1946), the First Piano Sonata (1946), and *Le visage nuptial* (*The Nuptial Countenance*, 1946–7) for chamber ensemble, including two *ondes Martenot*. In 1948 his talent was recognized with the Beethovenian Second Piano Sonata and the cantata *Le soleil des eaux* (*The Sun of the Waters*), based on poems by René Char. The

same year he began working on the "multiple choice" collection *Livre pour quatuor* for string quartet, to which he attempted to apply a technique of "total serialization". His most successful essay in this genre was *Structures I* (1952) for two pianos, but he quickly realized its limitations, and during the 1950s abandoned it in favour of freer techniques. He came to international attention in 1954 with *Le marteau sans maître* (*The Hammer without a Master*), settings of René Char poems for contralto and ensemble.

During the late 1950s and '60s Boulez taught at Darmstadt (an important centre of new music), Basle and Harvard. He also established a parallel career as a conductor. He was musical director of the BBC Symphony Orchestra (1971–5) and also of the New York

Philharmonic (1971–8), and was a sought-after guest conductor (he conducted Wagner's *Ring* cycle at Bayreuth in 1976, and the first production of Berg's *Lulu* in Paris). From 1977–92 he was the founder-director of the Institut de Recherche et de Coordination Acoustique/Musique (IRCAM) in Paris, which provides computers and digital facilities for composition. His most important later compositions – many of which are still being revised – include the Third Piano Sonata (1957), *Pli selon pli* (*Fold upon Fold*) for orchestra, *Eclat/Multiples* for ensemble, *Rituel in memoriam Bruno Maderna* (1974–5), two works called *Dérive* for small ensemble, *Domaines*, for clarinet and 22 instruments (1961–8); *...explosante-fixe...* (1971–89), and *Répons*, for ensemble including computers and live electronics.

ABOVE: *Boulez conducting Stravinsky's* The Rite of Spring *in 1963. Boulez never uses a baton to conduct.*

Life and works

NATIONALITY: French

BORN: Montbrison, 1925

SPECIALIST GENRES: Music for various instrumental and vocal ensembles, piano works.

MAJOR WORKS: *Structures I* and *II* (1952–61); *Le marteau sans maître* (1954); *Pli selon pli* (1957–90); *Répons* (1981); three piano sonatas.

Karlheinz Stockhausen

In Stockhausen's good period I came to trust his music more than anything else.

PIERRE BOULEZ (BORN 1925)

When electronic music seemed to represent the future in the 1960s and '70s, Stockhausen was at its cutting edge. He studied at the Cologne Musikhochschule after the war, and then went to Cologne University, where his analytical skills impressed everyone. In 1951 he met Messiaen at the Darmstadt summer school, and went to Paris to study with him; at the same time he made his first experiments with *musique concrète* in the electronic music studios of French radio.

In 1953 Stockhausen went back to Cologne, where he worked in

ABOVE: *Karlheinz Stockhausen (born 1928), one of the most influential German composers of the 20th century.*

the electronic music studio of West German Radio (he became its director ten years later), and also studied acoustics at Bonn University. By the late 1950s he was himself a sought-after teacher: he has taught at Darmstadt, at various American universities, and at the Cologne Musikhochschule, where he has been a professor of composition since 1971.

Like many later 20th-century composers, Stockhausen's starting point was the music of Webern. In his own works he attempted a process of

total serialization, of pitch, intensity, duration, timbre, and spatial position. He divided his compositions into "groups" or "moments" (as in *Momente*, 1961–4, for soprano, four chamber groups, and 13 instruments), and then experimented with varying the order of "groups" in performance (as in *Zyklus*, 1959, for percussion, and some of his *Klavierstücke* (*Piano Pieces*).

Since the 1970s Stockhausen has been working on a huge opera cycle called *Licht* (*Light*), one opera for each day of the week, which has spawned a series of related instrumental compositions.

ABOVE: *Stockhausen in the recording studio. Many of his compositions use electronic media.*

Life and works

NATIONALITY: German

BORN: Cologne, 1928

SPECIALIST GENRES: Serial and electronic music.

MAJOR WORKS: *Kontra-Punkte* (*Counter-points*, 1952–3); *Gruppen* (*Groups*) for three orchestras (1955–7); *Gesang der Jünglinge* (*Song of the Youths*, 1955–6); *Kontakte* (*Contacts*, 1959–60); *Stimmung* (*Mood*, 1968); *Ylem* (1972); *Aus dem sieben Tagen* (*From the Seven Days*, 1968).

Iannis Xenakis

Mathematics is music for the mind; music is mathematics for the soul.

ANONYMOUS

Iannis Xenakis was born in Romania, but his parents moved back to their native Greece when he was ten. He began studying music from the age of 12, but was trained as an engineer. During the war Xenakis fought in the Greek Resistance, losing an eye and narrowly escaping death. In 1947 he went to Paris, where he studied with Arthur Honegger and Darius Milhaud, and then with Messiaen in the early 1950s.

Between 1947 and 1960 he worked with the French avant-garde architect Le Corbusier (1887–1965), designing the much-admired Philips Pavilion for the 1958 Brussels Exhibition, in which Varèse's specially commissioned *Poème électronique* was played. Xenakis subsequently began to make his name as a composer, and thereafter concentrated on music. He has taught at Indiana University in the USA and also in Paris, where he was professor of music at the Sorbonne from 1972–89.

Xenakis's strong interest in mathematics led him to introduce mathematical concepts and theories into his compositions, some of which are scored for traditional instruments, others for electronic media. He applied the term "stochastic" to music, relating to the theory of probability, which assumes that a chance sequence of events can reach a predetermined conclusion. In his own works (many of which have Greek titles), the elements of chance are not left to the performer (as in works by Cage or Lutoslawski), but are controlled by the composer, normally by using a computer. Some of his earlier pieces, such as *Nomos gamma* (1967–8) place an orchestra among the audience. His later pieces vary in size from *Okho* (1989) for three players, to *Dox-Orkh* and *Troorkh* (both 1991), respectively for violin and trombone with 89 other players.

ABOVE: The works of Iannis Xenakis (1922–2001) are based on mathematical concepts and theories.

LEFT: Xenakis with one of his scores. He lost his sight in one eye while fighting in the Greek Resistance in 1947.

Life and works

NATIONALITY: Greek

BORN: Braïla, Romania, 1922; **DIED:** Paris, 2001

SPECIALIST GENRES: Compositions based on mathematical concepts.

MAJOR WORKS: *Metastasis* (1953–4); *Oresteia* (1965–6); *Terretektorh* (1965–6); *Persephassa* (1969).

Luciano Berio

Abstract it may be, the human voice…

THOMAS MANN (1875–1955), "DR FAUSTUS"

Together with Bruno Maderna (1920–73), with whom he founded the Studio di Fonologia Musicale at Radiotelevisione Italiana in Milan in 1955, Luciano Berio is one of the most important Italian composers of his generation. He studied at the Milan Conservatory, and has been equally active as both teacher and composer. He has taught composition at Tanglewood, Mills College, California, Harvard University and the Juilliard School in the USA, at Dartington in Britain and at Darmstadt and Cologne in Germany. In the late 1970s he also worked with Boulez at IRCAM in Paris.

Berio's compositions reflect his fascination with the human voice, intensified by his marriage (1950–66)

ABOVE: *Luciano Berio (born 1925), the major Italian composer of his generation.*

to the American singer/actress Cathy Berberian (1925–83). He draws inspiration from the juxtaposition of different musical processes, from Baroque vocal styles to modern techniques of serialism, indeterminacy and the use of electronics and computer technology. His idiomatic use of collage technique is demonstrated in his most popular work, *Sinfonia* for eight voices and orchestra, which quotes from a wide range of sources, including works by Mahler, Wagner, Ravel and Richard Strauss. He has also reworked music by Brahms and Schubert, most recently in *Rendering* (1989), attributed to "Schubert/Berio". Several of his pieces written for Cathy Berberian also use

collage technique, in particular *Recital I (for Cathy)*, for mezzo-soprano and 17 instruments (1972).

Among Berio's best-known works are the *Quattro canzoni popolari* for voice and piano (1946–7); *Circles*, based on poems by e. e. cummings, for female voice, harp and percussion; *O King* (a homage to Martin Luther King), for mezzo and five players (1967); the series of solo works called *Sequenze I–XI* (*No. III*, for voice, was written for Berberian); and a related series called *Chemins (Paths)* for solo instrument(s) and ensemble or orchestra. He has written several theatre works, some in collaboration with distinguished writers such as Italo Calvino and Umberto Eco.

ABOVE: *Berio rehearsing the BBC Symphony Orchestra in their Maida Vale recording studio in London, February 2000.*

Life and works

NATIONALITY: Italian

BORN: Oneglia, 1925

SPECIALIST GENRES: Works for both conventional and electronic media.

MAJOR WORKS: *Epifanie* (1959–61); *Circles* (1960); *Sinfonia* (1968–9); *Coro* (1975–6); *Un re in ascolto* (*King in Waiting*, 1979–83); 11 *Sequenze* (1958–75); four *Chemins* (*Paths*, 1965–75).

Hans Werner Henze

My profession…consists of bringing truths nearer to the point where they explode.

HENZE, "MUSIC AND POLITICS" (1982)

Henze was the eldest of six children of a schoolmaster, who discouraged him from taking up music. He began composing at 12, but received no formal musical training until after the war (during which he had been attached to a unit making Nazi propaganda films). In 1946 he began to study harmony and counterpoint with Wolfgang Fortner (born 1907), and serial techniques with René Leibowitz. In 1953, after finishing his first opera, *Boulevard Solitude*, he settled in Italy.

During the 1960s Henze's music became associated with radical, left-wing politics. He shot to international fame in 1966 when his opera *The Bassarids*, with a libretto by W. H. Auden and Chester Kallman, was produced at the

ABOVE: *Hans Werner Henze (born 1926), considered the major German opera composer of his generation.*

Salzburg Festival, and his 1968 oratorio *Das Floss der "Medusa"* (*The Raft of the "Medusa"*) – one of his best-known works – was written as a requiem for the guerrilla leader Che Guevara.

Henze also began to work with young musicians, and in 1976 founded the Montepulciano Cantiere in Umbria for communal international music-making. Since 1980 he has taught composition at the Cologne Academy and at the Royal Academy of Music in London, and in 1988 he founded the Munich International Festival of New Music Theatre. He combines composing with conducting, and has been a guest conductor of the Berlin Philharmonic Orchestra.

During the 1970s and '80s Henze collaborated with the British playwright Edward Bond on works such as the "action for music" *We Come to the River*, the ballet *Orpheus* (1979) and the opera *The English Cat* (1980–2). His highly coloured, richly orchestrated works include several operas, of which the early works *Der Prinz vom Homburg* (1958), *Elegy for Young Lovers* (1959–61) and *Der junge Lord* (*The Young Lord*, 1964) are perhaps the best known: the latest is *Venus and Adonis* (1993–5) for singers and dancers. A prolific composer for both instruments and voices, he has also written nine symphonies, two violin concertos, two piano concertos and other concertante works, five string quartets, several ballets, and a great deal of vocal music.

Life and works

NATIONALITY: German

BORN: Gütersloh, Westphalia, 1926

SPECIALIST GENRES: Opera and theatre music.

MAJOR WORKS:
Boulevard Solitude (1951); *König Hirsch* (*King Stag*, 1956); *The Bassarids* (1966); *Das Floss der "Medusa"* (1968); *We Come to the River* (1976).

ABOVE: *Hans Werner Henze at work in 1996.*

Other Composers of the Era

It is fortunate that to assert itself in music, a new generation does not need to destroy the works of its ancestors.

Ernst Křenek (1900–91), "Horizons Circled" (1974)

Although the demand for contemporary music is relatively limited compared with that of earlier periods, many talented composers have achieved widespread popularity over the last 50 years.

America

In the USA, a group of so-called "minimalists" came to attention in the 1970s and '80s. Among them is Steve Reich (born 1936), who founded his own ensemble in 1966. He was much influenced by African and Asian drumming techniques, and all his works, which range from vocal and orchestral pieces such as *The Desert Music* (1982–4) for 27 amplified voices and orchestra,

ABOVE: The American composer Steve Reich (born 1936) introduced the "phasing" technique, whereby instruments play the same patterns at slightly different speeds.

to the famous *Clapping Music* for two performers (1972), and *Different Trains* for string quartet and tape (1988), deal with *ostinato* patterns subtly altered by variations in time. Similar repetitive techniques govern the work of Terry Riley (born 1935), whose most famous piece is *In C* (1964).

Two other minimalists, Philip Glass (born 1937) and John Adams (born 1946) have developed the technique on a larger scale, including opera. Glass worked with Ravi Shankar (born 1920), and his style was influenced by Indian music. Of his many stage works, *Einstein on the Beach* (1974–5), *Akhnaten* (1980–3)

and *The Making of the Representative for Planet 8* (1988) are the best known; while his orchestral works include *Glassworks* (1981) for chamber orchestra, and a Third Symphony (1994). Adams's style is more eclectic, and he has a substantial international following. The subject-matter of both his operas, *Nixon in China* (1984–7) and *The Death of Klinghoffer* (1990–1), had contemporary resonance; while his *Grand Pianola Music* (1981–2) for two sopranos, two pianos and small orchestra, *The Wound Dresser* (1988–9) for baritone and orchestra, and his 1993 Violin Concerto have become widely known.

ABOVE: Philip Glass (born 1937), an American minimalist, has been influenced by Indian music.

ABOVE: John Adams (born 1946) successfully applied minimalist techniques to opera, including Nixon in China *(1984–7).*

ABOVE: *The Hungarian composer György Kurtág (born 1926) is a highly regarded teacher. His pupils have included the young British composer Thomas Adès.*

Central Europe and Russia

The (Romanian-born) Hungarian composer György Kurtág (born 1926), reared in the Bartók-Kodály tradition, has achieved international acclaim for his subtly crafted orchestral and chamber music, often making use of voices and cimbalom. Among his best-known works are *Messages of the Late Miss R.V. Troussova* (1976–80) for soprano and chamber ensemble, *…quasi una fantasia…* for piano and instruments (1987–8), *The Sayings* of *Péter Bornemisza* (1963–8) for soprano and piano, *Hommage à R. Sch.* for clarinet, viola and piano (1990), and the four books of *Games* for piano (1973–6).

The Polish composer Henryk Górecki (born 1933) draws his inspiration from a wide variety of sources: medieval Polish music, Renaissance polyphony, Webernian serialism, and Romantic orchestration. His serenely meditative Third Symphony (*Symphony of Sorrowful Songs*, 1976) was one of the few "classical" pieces to reach the charts.

A similar serenity pervades the sacred choral music of the Estonian composer Arvo Pärt (born 1935), who settled in West Berlin in 1980. His techniques embrace serialism and minimalism, but within an accessible idiom. His works include a St John Passion (1982), and the popular *Cantus in Memory of Benjamin Britten* for strings and bell (1977).

In the former USSR, Alfred Schnittke (born 1934) is held in high regard. His early works were influenced by serialism, and by the avant-garde techniques of Stockhausen and Ligeti, but he has produced a substantial body of work in traditional genres, including symphonies, *concerti grossi*, sonatas, trios and quartets. Together with Schnittke, Sofia Gubaidulina (born 1931) is the most important Russian composer of the present day. Born in Tatar, her work has been influenced by the exotic timbres of Caucasian folk music, and by a sensitive response to words.

Britain

The doyens of British music at the turn of the 21st century are Harrison Birtwistle and Peter Maxwell Davies (both born 1934), original members of the "Manchester School". Both have won wide acclaim, especially for their operas. Birtwistle has assumed the mantle of Britten and Tippett with an original series of theatre works, many inspired by myth. They include *Punch and Judy* (1966–7), *The Mask of Orpheus* (1973–84), *Gawain* (1987–94), *The Second Mrs Kong* (1993–4) and *The Last Supper* (2000), augmented by fine orchestral works including *The Triumph of Time* (1972), *Earth Dances* (1985–6) and *Endless Parade* for solo trumpet and strings (1986–7), written for the Swedish virtuoso Håkan Hardenberger (born 1961).

ABOVE: *The recording of Polish composer Henryk Górecki's Third Symphony (1977) was a surprise "hit".*

ABOVE: *The Russian composer Sofia Gubaidulina (born 1931). Her work is influenced by Caucasian folk music.*

ABOVE: *The doyen of contemporary British music – Harrison Birtwistle (born 1934), photographed in Los Angeles in 1994.*

In the 1960s Maxwell Davies founded the contemporary music ensemble The Fires of London (originally The Pierrot Players), for which he wrote theatre pieces such as *Eight Songs for a Mad King* (1969), and vocal and instrumental works such as *Revelation and Fall* for soprano and instruments (1966). The landscape and culture of the Orkney Islands, where he has lived since the 1970s, have inspired many of his later works, including the operas *The*

Martyrdom of St Magnus (1976–7), *The Lighthouse* (1979), and a series of *Strathclyde Concertos* for members of the Scottish Chamber Orchestra. He has written a great deal of music for children.

Many of Maxwell Davies' works spring from a religious impulse, as do all the later works of John Tavener (born 1944). Tavener derives his serene, meditative style from his Greek Orthodox faith, and has achieved fame with works such as *Ultimos ritos* (1972), *Resurrection* (1989), *Hymns of Paradise* (1992–3) and particularly *The Protecting Veil* for cello and strings (1987). He first attracted attention in the mid 1960s with his "crossover" cantata *The Whale*.

Several younger British composers promise exciting new developments in the 21st century. Among them are George Benjamin (born 1960), whose *Ringed by the Flat Horizon* (1979–80), *At First Light* (1982), and *A Mind of Winter* (1981) receive international performances. The Scottish composer James Macmillan (born 1959) came to prominence in 1990 with the orchestral work *The Confessions of Isobel Gowdie*, and has since produced an impressive body of work, largely inspired by his Catholicism.

ABOVE: *Peter Maxwell Davies (born 1934). Like Birtwistle, he was a member of the "Manchester School".*

Mark-Anthony Turnage (born 1960) draws inspiration from many sources including rock and jazz. His operas *Greek* (1986–8), *The Country of the Blind* (1997) and *The Silver Tassie* (2000) have received wide acclaim. Finally, Thomas Adès (born 1971), an extraordinarily talented prodigy, has won international awards for his fluent and characterful orchestral and chamber music. His first opera, *Powder Her Face* (1994–5), is being performed all over the world.

ABOVE: *The British composer John Tavener (born 1944). His works are strongly influenced by the Greek Orthodox tradition.*

ABOVE: *Mark-Anthony Turnage (born 1960), one of the rising stars of the younger generation of British composers.*

ABOVE: *The extraordinarily gifted young British composer Thomas Adès (born 1971) has won international acclaim.*

Glossary

Aleatoric music/aleatory: music in which random or chance elements are allowed to determine the course of the piece.

Aria: a lengthy and well developed solo vocal piece.

Atonal: not in any key.

Cantata: an extended choral work, usually with orchestral accompaniment.

Chromatic scale: a scale ascending or descending by semitones.

Clef: the sign that fixes the position of a particular note on the staff.

Coda: extra section at the end of a movement.

Concerto: a work for solo instrument(s) and orchestra, usually in three movements.

Counterpoint: the weaving together of two or more melodic lines to make musical sense, resulting in polyphony.

Development: in sonata form, the section of a movement following the initial statement of the themes, in which they are expanded or modified.

Exposition: the first part of sonata form, in which the main themes are stated.

Fugue: contrapuntal work in three or more parts of equal importance, which enter successively in imitation of each other.

Harmony: the simultaneous sounding of different notes.

Key: the classification of the notes of a scale, determined by the key-note.

Leitmotif: (leading motif) a short theme used repeatedly in a score – especially by Wagner – to denote an object, person or idea.

Libretto: the text of an opera or oratorio.

Minimalism: term applied to works based on the repetition of very short figures.

Mode: name for each of the ways of ordering the notes of a scale.

Monody: music on one line, without counterpoint or accompanying harmonies.

Motif, motive: a recognizable short group of notes in a work.

Motto theme: a theme that recurs during a piece of music, similar to a *Leitmotif.*

Musique concrète: music created on disc or tape by electronically modifying natural sounds.

Nocturne: a short lyrical piece, usually for piano.

Oratorio: an extended musical setting of a religious text in semi-dramatic form.

Ostinato: a persistently repeated phrase or rhythm.

Overture: (1) an orchestral opening movement to an opera, play or suite; (2) an orchestral work in one movement, usually with a title alluding to a literary or pictorial source.

Polytonality: the simultaneous use of more than one key.

Prelude: a musical introduction, or a short self-contained piece.

Programme music: a piece of music interpreting a picture or story.

Recapitulation: in sonata form, the section of a movement which repeats the original themes after the development.

Recitative: speech-like singing in opera used for dialogue or to precede an aria.

Serialism: technique whereby a structural "series" of notes governs the development of the composition.

Sonata: an instrumental work in three or four movements and for one or two players.

Sonata form: a construction used in the first movement of a sonata or symphony, which is divided into three sections: exposition, development and recapitulation.

Song-cycle: a set of songs grouped by the composer in a particular order for performance, often based on a sequence of poems.

Stochastic: a term denoting a process of which the steps are governed by rules of probability.

Suite: an instrumental piece in several movements.

Symphony: a substantial orchestral work, usually in four movements.

Tonality: the general key.

Tone cluster or note cluster: a group of adjacent notes played together.

Tone-poem: a substantial orchestral work intended to interpret a non-musical idea, picture or literary work.

Tone-row or note-row: a sequence of all 12 notes of the octave which forms the basis of a composition in 12-note music.

Trio: (1) a combination of three performers; (2) a work for three performers; (3) the centre section of a minuet, written in three parts.

Twelve-note system: the technique by which all 12 notes within an octave are treated as equal and placed in a particular order (note-row) to form the basis of the composition.

Index

Powell, Anthony 67, 68
Prokofiev, Sergei 18, 25,
64–5, 67, 69, 74, 75
Purcell, Henry 17, 78
Pushkin, Alexander 62

R
Rachmaninov, Sergei
26–7, 35
Ravel, Maurice **32–3**,
34, 37, 89
Reger, Max 52
Reich, Steve 7, 19, 72, **91**
Respighi, Ottorino **68**
Riley, Terry 72, **91**
Rimsky-Korsakov, Nikolay
17, 60, 68
Rodrigo, Joaquín **68**
Rossetti, Dante Gabriel 30
Rossini, Gioacchino 17,
68, 76
Rostropovich, Mstislav 65,
72, 77, 82
Rubinstein, Ida 33, 62

S
sacred music 54, 84
Satie, Erik **34**, 54, 69, 79
Scarlatti, Alessandro 14
Schnittke, Alfred **92**
Schoenberg, Arnold 6, 18,
19, 24, 25, 36, **48–9**, 50,
51, 52, 63, 79, 86
Schulhoff, Ervín **69**
Scriabin, Alexander **35**
Shankar, Ravi 91
Shostakovich, Dmitri 7, 18,
25, 64, 69, 72, **74–5**
Smetana, Bedřich 17, 40
Sondheim, Stephen 80
song-cycles 33, 76
Stalin, Joseph 65, 69, 74–5
Stanford, Charles Villers 37
stochastic composition 88
Stockhausen, Karlheinz 7,
25, 73, 84, **87**, 92

Strauss, Richard 17, 89
Stravinsky, Igor 7, 18, 25,
54, 56, **60–3**, 64, 74
Suk, Josef 40

T
Tavener, John **93**
Tchaikovsky, Pyotr Ilyich
60, 62
Tippett, Michael **78**
tonality 18, 24, 50, 72
tone-poems 38, 39, 41
Toscanini, Arturo 44, 59
Turnage, Mark-Anthony
72, **93**
twelve-note system 18,
24–5, 49, 86

V
Varèse, Edgard 7, 73, 88
Vaughan Williams, Ralph
6, 25, **37**, 38, 46
Verdi, Giuseppe 17, 76
Verlaine, Paul 24, 29

W
Wagner, Richard 17, 28–9,
32, 89
Walton, William 66, **67**
Warlock, Peter (Philip
Heseltine) 67, **69**
Webern, Anton 24, 48,
50, **52**, 83, 87
Weill, Kurt 25, **53**
Weir, Judith 73
Wittgenstein, Paul 33, 64

X
Xenakis, Iannis 72, 84, **88**

Y
Yevtushenko, Yevgeny 75

Z
Zverev, Nikolay 26, 35
Zweig, Stefan 50

Acknowledgements

The publisher would like to thank the following picture libraries for the use of their pictures in the book (l=left, r=right, t=top, b=bottom, m=middle).

Every effort has been made to acknowledge the pictures properly; however, we apologize if there are any unintentional omissions, which will be corrected in future editions.

AKG, London: 2; 15t; 16t; 25bl; 30t; 63b; *British Library* 10r; *Marion Kalter* 36b; 83t; 88t, b; *Erich Lessing* 16b; 50bl.
Arena Images Ltd: *Ron Scherl* 91br; *Colin Willoughby* 80b.
Art Archive Ltd: 15b.
Bridgeman Art Library, London: 6b; 14; 17b; 18; 22–3; 24t, b; 28t, bl, br; 29b; 31tl, b; 32t; 34t; 48t; 54b; 84t; *Giraudon* 33t; *Novosti* 26t.
Camera Press: 62bl, br; 69bl; 72t, b; 76t; 92t; *Karsh* 53t; 54t; 59t; 61t; *Patraig O'Donnell* 82t.
Eye Ubiquitous: *James Davis* 74br.
Frank Lane Picture Agency Limited: *H. D. Brandl* 85b.
Getty: 27; 38b; 48bl; 49; 57t, bl; 59b.

Hulton Getty: 57br; 68br; 84b.
Lebrecht Music Collection: 6t; 10l; 11tr, b; 12; 13l, r; 17l, tr; 26bl, br; 25t, br; 29t; 30b; 32bl; 33b; 34b; 35; 36t; 37; 38t; 39; 40t, bl, br; 41b; 42b; 43tl, tr, b; 44t; 45t, b; 46t, b; 47t; 48br; 50t; 51b; 52t, b; 55t, bl, br; 56t, b; 58t, b; 61bl; 63t; 64; 65tl, tr; 66; 67b; 69tl, tr, br; 75t, b; 92bl; *G. Anderhub* 7bl; *Archive Manuel de Falla* 68bl; *Milein Cosman* 60b; *Mike Evans* 78t, b; *David Farrell* 67t; 80t; 93tr; *Betty Freeman* 3; 73tl; 81t; 93tl; *Joanne Harris* 44b; *Matti Kolho* 65b; *Kurt Weill Foundation* 53b; *Andre LeCoz* 86b; *Nigel Luckhurst* 76b; 90b; *Suzie Maeder* 81b; 82b; 85t; *Kate Mount* 19t; 73tr; 79b; *Wladimir Polak* 77b; *Private Collection* 41t; 50br; 68t; *Mary Robert* 19bl; *Zsuzsi Roboz* 42t; *Celene Rosen* 11tl; *G. Salter* 77t; 83b; *D. Smirnov* 92br; *Richard H. Smith* 1; 86t; 89b; *Horst Tappe* 7tl; 60t; *Greg Tomin* 74t, bl; *Guy Vivien* 32br; *Toby Wales* 73b.
Performing Arts Library: 31tr; *Clive Barda* 51t; 79t; 87t, b; 89t; 90t; 91t, bl; 93bl, br; *Ben Christopher* 93bm; *Fritz Curzon* 19br; *Linda Rich* 61br; 62t.
The Stock Market: 47b; 70–1.